God's Panoply:
The Armour of God &
the Kiss of Heaven

God's Panoply

© Anne Hamilton 2015

Published by Armour Books
P. O. Box 492, Corinda QLD 4075

Cover by Anne Hamilton

ISBN: 978-1-925380-01-9

Originally published by Even Before Publishing in 2013
ISBN: 978-1-921633-01-0

National Library of Australia Cataloguing-in-Publication entry : (paperback)
Author: Hamilton, Anne, 1954- author.
Title: God's panoply : the armour of god : the kiss of heaven /
                 Anne Hamilton.
Edition: 2nd
ISBN: 9781925380019 (paperback)
Subjects: Spiritual warfare.
                 Marriage--Religious aspects--Christianity.
Dewey Number: 235.4

God's Panoply:
The Armour of God &
the Kiss of Heaven

Anne Hamilton

Contents

Foreword

If ever you've read a Japanese short story or ventured into manga or anime, you'll be aware it's an enigmatic world where the canons of western literature do not apply. A conflict-driven plot which heads towards a logical and satisfying resolution seems so natural to westerners after centuries of European story-telling that we unthinkingly assume the model must hold everywhere.

However the essence of Japanese literature and film-making is the evocation of a mood, the urge to encapsulate and convey a feeling. It strives to appeal to the senses, not the rational mind.

The Japanese have a concept, *utsuroi*, relating the notion of courage to beauty. Utsuroi, *point-of-change*, locates beauty at the moment of transition. The highest pleasure in the exquisite loveliness of the cherry blossom is the knowledge of its fleeting nature. Utsuroi is found in fugitive shapes, leaping shadows, the dappling of sunlight through leaves. 'It depends on an understanding that time is not linear nor one event after another in a chain, but an overlapping sequence of the same shapes and a shaken kaleidoscope.'[1]

This book is designed with extraordinary care. It uses an

ancient style which has as many names as there are researchers into its techniques. The name I have chosen to adopt is 'numerical literary design'. Despite this care, it is not linear in format. It is like a kaleidoscope.

Much of the book focuses on Hebrew thinking—which is making a resurgence in many places as Christians become more aware of the influence of Greek rationalism on the interpretation of Scripture. One thing I wanted to do with this book was to be very sure I did not take the usual linear logical approach: to approach Hebrew thought through a Greek cultural mechanism seems ironic and counter-productive.

The shaking of the kaleidoscope means that sometimes a line of thought may vanish for a while before it reappears. Such an approach may well take you out of your comfort zone, so please accept my apologies in advance.

Anne Hamilton

Prologue

WHEN ALEXANDER WAS NEARLY THREE, he called himself 'Xander'.

One Saturday morning, his dad said, 'Come on, Alexander. We're going to your favourite place—the hardware store.' Dad grimaced. 'That new sander is useless. I'm going to take it back and get a replacement.'

With a shriek, Alexander fled to his room and crawled under his bed. Great hiccupping sobs burst out of him. Every time his dad tried to coax him out, he'd wail and shrink back further against the wall.

'What's wrong, Alexander?' dad asked over and over again. 'Don't you want to come to the hardware store?'

Finally, Alexander's sobs calmed to snuffles and sniffles. 'Pwease, dad, I'll be good. I pwomise. Don't repwace me.'

At last Dad realised just what the problem was. Alexander had confused the words 'sander' and 'Xander'. Lots of cuddles and explanation later, he was quite happy to go off with Dad to their favourite place.

Xander laughed and giggled as he explored the hardware store and Dad got his new sander.

The limits of my language mean the limits of my world.

When Alexander was nearly six, his mum and dad adopted a little boy from South-East Asia. Nikolas was nearly three when he left the orphanage. Unable to speak except for a few grunts and wuffling burbles, he worried his new parents. Was he deaf? Or was something else wrong?

At nearly three, his brother might have confused 'sander' and 'Xander' but he'd had a wide vocabulary and he'd been noisily articulate. So Mum took Nikolas to a paediatrician.

'Nothing to worry about,' the specialist said. 'He's doing well in the circumstances. Babies don't learn to speak until they are spoken to. In an orphanage, he will have heard voices around him but not directed at him. He will have been spoken of, spoken over and spoken around—but probably never spoken to.'

Never spoken *to*.

As I consider the manifold staggering implications of this statement—that, to begin with, human beings do not learn language except through intentional and individual communication—my mind is drawn back through time.

How did the very first humans learn? Who taught them? What was the language of Eden?

Toddlers are usually eager to imitate the speech of their parents, building a slow lisping vocabulary and experimenting with grammatical structure. I recall one of my nieces, on being instructed to 'be good and behave', pouting: 'I am being good and I am being have.'

You'd think that, after our new birth while we are still spiritual babies, we'd be raring to re-learn the language of Eden. However, in this post-Babel century, that's not the case.

We're happy to remain like newborns, snuggling into the warm comforting idea the language of heaven is love.

But love is a verb.

It's also the context of the language, not the words themselves. The fact is, most of us don't want to take our first steps with any celestial tongue. We resist the very idea the language of heaven has a unique grammar or mode of thought. We know that God understands English so we don't exert ourselves to put aside our babytalk.

Few of us consider that there are concepts so foreign to our culture there are no words for them in English. Even if that thought crosses our minds, we'd rather be cosseted like infants than struggle with the sort of intentional and individual communication which originated in Eden.

What if we hear God wrong? What if we hear 'Xander' when He's said 'sander'?

We simply don't want to be mortified by those silly mistakes that happen when we don't quite understand what our Father is saying.

No doubt I will make some of those mistakes in this book. I've tried to go places where writers haven't been for centuries and I'm not sure I will always have my facts right. So I hope my mistakes will be endearingly childlike rather than embarrassingly childish.

The important thing is not to be totally right but to start the dialogue.

And, as I do, I make no apology for introducing some archaic words into this book. Words like *panoply*, *aweful* and *troth*. They might be obscure but they are largely free of modern cultural encrustation.

It's easier to learn the sense of a new word than unlearn that of an old familiar one. Nonetheless there are some old words that really do need addressing. So make yourself comfortable in God's lap or by His side—anywhere you can hear Him speak to you.

Not over you. Or around you. Or about you.

To you.

Because we're going to start with the hard stuff. We need to begin with the realisation this is not just a different language but an entirely different way of thinking.

1

Cover me

THE MĀORI PEOPLE OF AOTEAROA, the land of the long white cloud, had no word for forgiveness. *Utu*, payback, was so much a part of their tribal way of life that the concept was simply unimaginable.

As a result, missionaries to New Zealand in the nineteenth century were faced with an immense cultural obstacle: how could they explain God's love for all humanity? And portray His forgiveness of sin? How could they make comprehensible the life and death and resurrection of Jesus when reconciliation was such an alien concept?

They were required to develop far more than a new word for a vocabulary list, they needed to introduce an entirely different way of thinking. The concept of forgiveness was so foreign in Polynesian culture that no pre-existing word could be adapted to Christian use—the whole idea and its background had to be very carefully interpreted.

This situation was far from unique. It's occurred many times across the centuries.

The Vikings also found the concept of forgiveness incomprehensible. For them, *hefna sinum* was not simply payback, it was about a duty to avenge. Family members were obligated to uphold the honour of their kinsmen—whatever the consequence, whatever the inconvenience or cost. Feuds would escalate to involve relatives and friends. They would pass from one generation to another.

The sagas of the Norsemen show an increasing realisation over time that *hefna sinum* was completely futile. However, the stories also recognise that no one quite knew how to bring the practice to an end.

It is from *hefna sinum* we get our English word, 'sin'.

In our language, the word 'sin' has its roots in ideas of *revenge* and *unforgiveness*. In both Hebrew and Greek, the words for 'sin' have the sense of *missing the mark, falling short, going astray*.

Yet there's a certain genius in choosing *hefna sinum* to translate *chata'*. In English, *missing the mark* does not have the same aweful sense of an unholy fall that lies behind the Jewish thought.

There's blood between us, love, my love,
There's father's blood, there's brother's blood;
And blood's a bar I cannot pass:
I choose the stairs that mount above,
Stair after golden skyward stair,
To city and to sea of glass.

Christina Rossetti, *The Convent Threshold*

On quite a number of occasions I've been astonished to hear a sermon built around a definition of a word from the Oxford English Dictionary. The preacher simply picked up a word from a verse in one translation of Scripture and teased out its meaning.

Jorge Luis Borges lays bare the uncontested assumption behind such an approach: *'The dictionary is based on the hypothesis— obviously an unproven one—that languages are made up of equivalent synonyms.'*

The possibility that such a sermon could just as easily miss the mark completely as hit the target doesn't seem to cross the mind of such preachers. Just because it's possible to score a bullseye with words like 'atonement' (*at–one–ment*, from *to set at one* or *be reconciled*) doesn't guarantee future success.

We often forget that, except in a very few isolated instances, we don't have a record of what Jesus actually said. In part, a red-letter Bible fosters the illusion that we are just one step away from the exact wording. However we really don't know precisely what He said for the very simple reason the Greek New Testament rarely gives us the original Aramaic.

There are a few occasions when it does. For instance—

To the daughter of Jairus: 'Talitha, cumi.' *Little girl, arise.*[2]

To Simon, son of Jonah: 'Cephas.' *Peter, the rock.*[3]

To Abba Father: 'Eloi, eloi, lama sabachthani.'[4] *My God, My God, why have You forsaken me?*[5]

However these instances are so uncommon it is fair to say the Gospels are already translations. Aramaic Hebrew has been rendered in koine Greek.

This is not a problem, of course, if the two languages have exactly corresponding thoughtforms and precisely equivalent words.

But what if there were subtle shades of difference? Or gaps that were the result of cultural imperatives like *utu* or *hefna sinum*? What if there were words with a sense totally at variance with the original?

The big problem is, of course, that this was not a 'what if' situation at all.

The original is unfaithful to the translation.

Jorge Luis Borges

'*Wives, submit to your husbands.*'

Before you have a Xander moment and dive under your bed to sob your heart out, please bear with me.

Paul of Tarsus has a very poor reputation in many circles for this instruction. How such a die-hard romantic could have been so misunderstood is quite beyond me at times. This single direction of his in Ephesians 5:22 has caused untold heart-searching and anguish in many women. In some men, intense anger has culminated in brutal physical abuse because, for them, this verse is a mandate excusing the violent crushing of a woman's will.

Nineteenth century New Zealand missionaries confronted with *utu* had a massive translation problem. However it was relatively simple compared to the issues Paul faced in the first century.

It's one thing when there is no word. It's entirely another when the best word has a diametrically opposite meaning to the original. In that case, of course, a good translator would go out of his way to clarify—across several paragraphs, if necessary—his language choice.

Paul, being altogether thorough, did exactly this. He knew he had to explain the Hebrew thought underlying the Greek word for 'submit'. Even so, because we've forgotten this is a translation, we've often focussed on the fine nuances of the Greek text instead of looking behind it to Hebrew thought and behind even that to the language of heaven.

The Greek word for 'submit' in this verse is *hupotasso*. It has military overtones. The same word is used in Romans 13 where Paul discusses submitting to the governing powers. There his extended passage on obedience to rulers and authorities segues into some thoughts on love and relationships before he abruptly changes the topic and brings in the armour of light.

In Ephesians 5, after telling wives to submit to their husbands, he moves onto some thoughts about love and relationships before he abruptly changes the topic and brings in the armour of God.

There's a distinctive pattern in both cases:

SUBMISSION ➜ LOVING RELATIONSHIPS ➜ ARMOUR

Once we have two similar instances like this, we should immediately suspect 'armour' is not an abrupt change of subject but part of a natural thought sequence.

Is there a Hebrew word covering just this territory? In fact there is: it's *nasa'*.

Like *hupotasso*, it has a military flavour. It is rich with other overtones too but only the martial ones concern us at the moment. Like *hupotasso*, it's about submission.

However, *nasa'* and *hupotasso*, for all their similarity of meaning, are also at odds. The Hebrew concept of submission is not even remotely like the Greek one. The Greek idea of submission resonates with the idea of *putting down*, while the Hebrew is wholly about *lifting up*.

'*Wives, lift up your husbands. Be their companions for battle.*'

It's such a provocative translation we'd have to be very sure Paul intended it from the beginning.

I think we can be.

I'll lift you and you lift me, and we'll both ascend together.

John Greenleaf Whittier

Let's cast our minds back over three thousand years. It's the Bronze Age. We're looking down on a small country on the eastern shores of the Mediterranean Sea. Early morning light is spearing through a red ruffling of clouds as we zoom in on a tall well-built man sitting under a pomegranate tree.

He looks depressed. As well he might. He's about to fight a battle and, apart from himself and his son, none of his troops have armour. The enemy has made sure his people have no access to metal or a blacksmith's forge.

Devising a battleplan in these circumstances is far from ideal. To make matters worse, there's an enemy garrison stationed on a nearby ridge. The man's frustrations boil over as his troops dwindle, quietly deserting their countrymen in the night. He's desperate. He needs God on-side.

The man is a king.

He's preoccupied. He's just waited a week for a prophet to arrive to offer sacrifices to ensure victory. All that time, he's watched his troops grow increasingly restless. Panicking, he'd just offered the sacrifices himself. The prophet had arrived the moment he finished and told him his presumption would mean the loss of his kingdom.

His mind is so busy thinking up new ways to placate God and turn the situation around he doesn't notice two significant men are missing.

On morning parade, his orders are strict: on pain of death, everyone must fast until victory is declared. He scowls, knowing the men are grumbling in their hearts even if they haven't said a word. He feels he can hear their thoughts: *who does Saul think he is to tell*

God's Panoply

us to go without food and fight without weapons?

Let's shift our attention now and take a long view up the valley towards those missing men. One of them is Prince Jonathan. The other is his bodyguard and he's the one we're actually interested in.

No—not Jonathan, not Saul. Our focus is on this unnamed soldier, known only as 'the armour-bearer'.

Obviously Jonathan's life was in this man's charge and he would have been willing to lay down his life to protect him. His title comes from the word *nasa', to bear* or *to lift up*, and he is one of the first of the great warrior company which includes David, Jesus and the Holy Spirit.

Now Jonathan's trust in God is in marked contrast to that of his father. He's not worried about troop numbers, nor buying God's favour with a sacrifice or a fast, nor even with auspicious timing. 'Tell you what,' he confides to his armour-bearer. 'Let's go buzz the Philistines. If they say, "We're coming down to get you," we'll make ourselves scarce, but if they say, "Come on up so we can teach you a lesson," that'll be the sign God has given them into our hands.'

The next statement gives us the only words from the armour-bearer actually recorded in Scripture. Since he's our real focal point, they are incredibly important.

'Do whatever is in your heart. I am with you soul and mind.'

I am with you.

Heart, soul and mind.

It was common practice for an armour-bearer to be a blood-brother to the person he'd sworn to protect. They had sworn oaths to each other and, as a consequence, their souls were knitted together. The armour-bearer was in complete submission but it was a submission to someone now closer than a brother. Someone as close as his own soul.

It was the deepest expression of friendship.

Such submission primarily meant mutual lifting and uplifting—physically, emotionally and spiritually. It involved initiative, enterprise and discernment—and sometimes rescue. It did not mean blind obedience.

Such unswerving commitment and loyalty changes the odds. GK Chesterton expresses it brilliantly in *The Man Who Was Thursday*: '...there are no words to express the abyss between isolation and having one ally. It may be conceded to the mathematicians that four is twice two. But two is not twice one; two is two thousand times one.'

There are special rules of multiplication heaven brings to bear when faith is allied with mutuality.

Jonathan and his armour-bearer tapped into it when, together, they scaled a cliff and took out a contingent of Philistines. They began a rout that Saul and his troops were then able to use to their advantage.

Many centuries later, Paul the apostle recognised the precise battleplan that won the day. Thinking of the words of Jonathan's armour-bearer, he wrote, *'Wives, submit to your husbands,'* meaning *lift them up, be their companions for battle.* It's why his thoughts turn just a few paragraphs later to divine armour.

Great men hallow a whole people, and lift up all who live in their time.

Sydney Smith

In the Hebrew understanding of the Scriptures, there are four levels of interpretation.

- **Pashat** = *plain*, the obvious and surface meaning.
- **Remez** = *hint*, the deeper meaning; just beyond the literal.
- **Derash** = *inquiry*, the comparative, sifted meaning.
- **Sod** = *secret*, the meaning given through inspiration or revelation.

Now, as we progress, we're going to move from pashat to remez, using all of the hints that Paul has left lying around. The symbols he used in the last two chapters of Ephesians point to a hidden layer. In fact, when it comes to the armour of God, there are at least two hidden layers. These sub-surface features offer up to us some exceptionally fine clues about what's really going on in plain sight.

But, before we start digging, we really need to grasp what an armour-bearer is.

Now modern descriptions tend to equate an armour-bearer to an errand-boy. Someone who runs messages, keeps your gear in good order and picks up after you. To be honest, I'm not sure how many errand-boys are willing to die for their boss.

Other descriptions liken an armour-bearer to an executive's personal assistant. Closer perhaps; I'm not sure how many PAs are willing to serve their bosses for the rest of their lives, even without pay.

Still other descriptions suggest the best parallel for an armour-bearer is a bodyguard. Nearer still; however I'm not altogether sure how many bodyguards would, if their boss died, adopt his family.

The fact is, none of these descriptions really come close to the idea of an armour-bearer. According to Graham Cooke, its essential meaning is *the one who covers the head*.[6] The one who stands in harm's way to protect you and keep you from danger. The one who, when you need cover in the battles of life, is always there for you, no questions asked.

This would seem to suggest that there is no modern equivalent to an armour-bearer. And perhaps there isn't, outside of literature.

The hero of the most popular book[7] of the twentieth century—

JRR Tolkien's *The Lord of The Rings*—fits perfectly into the archetype of an armour-bearer.

I belong to that minority of readers who finished Tolkien's trilogy and was a bit puzzled. I thought that Sam was the real hero. Sam—the quiet and unassuming hobbit, the gardener who became a Ringbearer—surely it was his unflinching loyalty that made the ultimate difference? Surely it was his unswerving integrity that, more than once, kept the quest from abysmal failure? A servant to Frodo, he was also his friend.

Everything that Sam stands for is epitomised by his agonising trek up the slopes of Mount Doom, carrying Frodo on his back.

To me, it was therefore always a bit disappointing to find Sam only truly coming into his own—and into the foreground as well—on the very last page. Until then he was always overshadowed by Frodo and Strider, Gandalf and Galadriel and even Merry and Pippin.

So it was with delighted surprise I discovered Tolkien himself considered Sam to be the trilogy's real hero. The character was written to pay homage to a group of people whose courage and sacrifice during the First World War Tolkien felt had been universally overlooked: an officer's batman.

It's in Sam we see not only the armour-bearer but the ideal of submission. It's not mindless obedience. It's about having initiative, carrying others, lifting them up when they fall, keeping faith: like Ruth with Naomi, *'Where you go, I will go; where you lodge, I will lodge; your people shall be my people, and your God my God.'*[8] It's about a friendship that lays everything on the line.

Everything.

'A gift for a gift,' said Kamal straight; 'a limb for the risk of a limb. Thy father has sent his son to me, I'll send my son to him!'

With that, he whistled his only son, that dropped from a mountain-crest—
He trod the ling like a buck in spring, and he looked like a lance at rest.
'Now here is thy master,' Kamal said, 'who leads a troop of the Guides,
And thou must ride as his left side as shield on shoulder rides.
Till Death or I cut loose the tie, at camp and board and bed,
Thy life is his—thy fate it is to guard him with thy head.'

Rudyard Kipling, *The Ballad of East and West*

Jonathan had his armour-bearer. So did his father Saul. In fact, Saul had several armour-bearers. One of them was David.

The interactions between David and Saul can only be understood by realising David was the 'keeper of his head', the one to whom Saul could say, 'Cover me,' on going into battle.

They had cut a covenant relationship; sworn oaths and solemnised their blood brotherhood by a ritual ceremony. Saul violated this covenant at every turn; David kept it even when he was under considerable pressure not to.

When you look at the full panorama of David's life, it's hard to understand why he was called 'a man after God's own heart'. However I think the key lies in his relationship with Saul and Jonathan. The Lord God is a covenant-keeping God. David, for all his many faults and failings, was a covenant-keeping man.

When Saul became sufficiently jealous of David to want to kill him, he chased him over hills and through valleys, out into the desert and back again. At one point, David was hiding in a cave when Saul came in, alone, to relieve himself. The opportunity was so obvious that David's men urged him to kill Saul: in their view, it was clear God had orchestrated the moment. It is also clear from

David's words that he was thinking of the covenant between them when he refused. 'Far be it from me,' he said, 'to *lift up my hand against* the Lord's anointed.'

The task of an armour-bearer, indeed his identity as his Hebrew name attested, was *to lift up on behalf of* another; therefore to lift up against another was not just to break his word and taint his honour, it was to strike at his own heart.

Years later, when Saul is fatally wounded in the battle at Mount Gilboa, he asks his new armour-bearer to put an end to his life. The man can't do it; the internal conflict is too huge: he has sworn an oath to die for Saul, not kill him.

David's lament when he hears of the deaths of Saul and Jonathan has no sense of relief that his own years of exile are finally over. He had been in covenant relationship with both of them—they were 'heart of his own heart', their souls had been knitted together, they were one.

As far as David was concerned, the day Saul and Jonathan died was the day a part of himself died too. Yet he was still concerned to keep his covenant with them by looking out for their families.

Why was this covenant so serious? It's nothing like the contracts of today which might prescribe penalty clauses if you don't keep them. It's far deeper, far more solemn, far more serious. In ancient Israel, you didn't make a covenant, you *cut* one. The sevenfold ceremony involved:

- The sacrifice of an animal
- The walk of blood
- The cutting of palms or wrists
- The exchange of weapon belts
- The exchange of mantles
- The exchange of names
- The covenant meal

Each of these actions was symbolic of two people becoming one.[9] The concept of such a covenant was not restricted to the Jews.

Henry Clay Trumball points to similar rites of blood brotherhood existing throughout the world, even into the late nineteenth century. In some cultures, the 'oneness' of blood brothers was sufficient cause to forbid them to marry each others' sisters. Nor, in a number of places, were there gender restrictions. A man and a woman could have a covenant—it was normal for that to be marriage, but it didn't have to be.

It was even possible, so the Hebrews maintained, to have a covenant with God.

> *'For there is no friend like a sister*
> *In calm or stormy weather...*
> *To lift one if one totters down*
> *To strengthen whilst one stands.'*

Christina Rossetti, Goblin Market

My armour-bearer is the *keeper of my head* or *the one who covers my head* or sometimes even just simply *my head*. He's my helmet, my shield, my covering, my standard-bearer, my banner, the one who loves me enough to lay down his life for me.

In English, we tend to think of 'head' in reference to a person at the top, the leader, the chief, the one who has precedence, the one who comes first, the one in charge and giving commands, the one to be obeyed without question.

However does Paul mean it like this? When he used the term

'head' straight after the in/famous instruction, *'Wives, submit to your husbands,'* did he have in mind our current understanding of 'first and foremost'? Or was he primarily thinking of 'head' in terms of a defender, a kinsman-redeemer, a helmet of salvation, a shield and covering, a keeping power?

Since he went immediately on to speak of Christ as the *'head of the Church'* coupling that with *'saviour of the body,'*[10] I have to suspect he was thinking of the ancient concept of an armour-bearer, not the modern idea of a president. Rather than a leader who issues orders, I believe he was harking back to the Hebrew idea of the covenant defender: the man prepared to lay down his life on behalf of his bride, just as Jesus laid down his life on behalf His bride, the church.

Back in his first letter to the Corinthians, Paul gives us more of his thoughts on man as the head of woman.[11] I don't want to lay too much stress on this passage because, at this point, Paul's rhetoric is tangled and his logic tortured. Obviously the background of these verses was familiar to both himself and his readers: they knew what we do not about his assumptions.

Several things are, however, clear:

- 'head' may or may not be used in the sense of 'leader' but it is definitely used in the sense of 'covering'
- when it comes to praying or prophesying (times of spiritual battle), the covering of the head is important
- when it comes to praying or prophesying (times of spiritual battle), there are different requirements for men and women regarding this symbolic covering of the head[12]
- the reason for the covering has something to do with the glory inherent in a head or its covering

Although I cannot be certain, I have to suspect the Greek word translated 'glory' equated in the back of Paul's mind—at least in this instance—to 'dignity'. Both of these are concepts which, in Hebrew thought, were connected with *weight*—with *gravity* in both its sense of solemnity and reverence and also its sense of heaviness.

During the cutting of a covenant, mantles were exchanged. Mantles were symbolic of dignity, of authority and, of course, of destiny. By giving one to another person, you would confer on them your own dignity and authority. Even today we speak of 'passing the mantle' in the sense of authorising a successor and handing on a specific legacy and destiny.

As time passed by, but particularly after the Babylonian captivity, the mantles people wrapped around themselves were, at times, conflated with the cloths wrapped around the head: turbans.

Thus when Paul speaks of glory connected with the head, I think he is thinking of this covering which symbolised dignity and was an essential element of covenant exchange. I put down much of the convolution of his thought, in this letter to the Corinthians, to the multiple exchanges of dignity resulting from multiple covenants: man with God, God with woman, and woman with man. It's not a simple linear process.

It's one of those things in Hebrew that is simply not easy to explain.

The very first word for God in the Bible is another one of them: *elohim*.

It's a plural word, hinting from the start at the Trinitarian nature of the divine. It's a masculine word, hinting at a father–son relationship within the godhead.

But one thing not often mentioned about it is this: its form is unique. It is a masculine plural of a feminine singular.

Try as hard as I can to wrap my thinking around that mind-warping concept, I can't. It's too deep and wide, high and stunning for me.

Let me return to simpler concepts of male and female. Back in the fifth chapter of his letter to the Ephesians where he speaks of the husband as the head of his wife, Paul immediately goes on to the analogy of the sacrificial love Christ demonstrated for His bride, the church.

From this point forward, as more and more ideas of mutuality are discussed, Paul repeatedly brings in ideas of the covenant defender. Surely it's so that his Greek readers, even if they had taken the wrong sense of 'hupotasso', *submit*, would eventually get the message.

Even the Greeks would not have thought of taking a single sentence, ignoring its context and the word–number fusion surrounding it, and puffing it up the way we so often do today. Certainly rabbi Paul, the descendant of the tribe of Benjamin, wouldn't have. Because there's a very good reason he talks about husbands and wives in terms of armour-bearing. And it has to do with a Hebrew word for marriage.

Praise to the Lord who in all things is wondrously reigning and, as on wings of an eagle, uplifting, sustaining...

Joachim Neander
tr. Catherine Winkworth

One of the Hebrew words for married—*nasu*—is derived from *nasa', to lift up*. This automatically makes it kin to armour-bearer. It is also kin to *nissi*, a *standard* or a *banner*.

In traditional Jewish weddings, the couple are lifted up on chairs as a symbol of God's intention for marriage. It is designed as an institution of mutual uplift hallowed by Jehovah Nissi—*the lord my banner*—who is a witness to the vows of the covenanting couple. The pavilion where the bridegroom waits for the bride is symbolic

God's Panoply

of the divine banner: *He brought me to his banqueting house and his banner over me was love*, wrote Solomon in Song of Songs,[13] a sensual celebration of the delight, passion and yearning of marital love.

God was first revealed as Jehovah Nissi during the time the Israelites wandered in the desert. In Exodus 17, the Amalekites attack the camp and Moses sends Joshua to mount a counter-attack. Moses then *lifts up* his hands to heaven and, as he is praying, the Israelites prevail. But as his arms grow weary and his hands drop, the tide of battle turns. Aaron and Hur stand at his sides, *lifting up* his arms until such time as the Amalekites are totally defeated.

The Lord my banner refers to the God who covers us in battle as we lift up our hands in prayer and praise. It refers to working together as one team. Joshua couldn't do it alone. He couldn't fight the battle without divine help and that required Moses to keep calling on the name of the One who lifts up, carries His people in battle and bears them safely through the day of conflict. However Moses couldn't do it alone, either. He couldn't be a rallying point when he was dropping with fatigue. Consequently he was dependent on Aaron. And even Aaron couldn't do his bit alone: he needed help from Hur.

It should come as no real surprise to us that *nasu*, married, derives from a word first used in warfare. A banner is part of the panoply—the armour—of a warrior; it's a rallying point and a standard, floating high above the battlefield. This is why marriage partners are called into submission: so they can lift each other up above the conflicts of life, carry each other when the battle is too intense and bear them safely through until the trouble is over.

The very word for marriage in Hebrew tells us there's more to it than mutual uplift. Its ultimate origin reveals that husband and wife are meant to be—as Paul hinted by using the military term *hupotasso* in 'Wives, submit to your husbands'—each other's companion for battle. They are called to be each other's armour-bearer.

I sometimes think it's a real pity Paul didn't consult his fellow-apostles on the subject.

John had a much better idea on how to translate *armour-bearer* into Greek.

A person standing alone can be attacked and defeated, but two can stand back-to-back and conquer. Three are even better, for a triple-braided cord is not easily broken.

Ecclesiastes 4:12 NLT

The Roman army had a square battle formation. When this square was broken by an enemy attack, they followed a trick they'd learned from the Greeks. Moving into pairs, they would fight back-to-back. Their armour—their helmets, shields, breastplates and swords—protected them in front. Their backs were protected by the companion behind them.

Should either be cut down, the other would move to defend him by straddling his fallen body and continuing the fight. In essence, they filled for each other a role similar to the Hebrew armour-bearer. However covenantal friendship—oneness—was not necessarily involved. Still, some sense of it remained in the mutual obligation soldiers often felt towards those who had saved their lives.

According to John Sandford, when the battle was over, the soldier still standing would bear his companion off the field and tend to his injuries.[14]

The ancient Greek name for this battle companion was the *paraclete.*

God's Panoply

נשׁא

A true friend never gets in your way unless you happen to be going down.

Arnold Glasgow

 נשׁא

A courtroom is in a sense a battleground. The usual translation of *paraclete* as 'advocate' gives legal overtones to what is essentially a term of warfare.[15]

I suspect that, in his description of the armour of God, Paul actually implies the presence of the paraclete: he mentions no covering for the back whatsoever.

Yet in a deep layer of the passage—a *remez*, a hint, within the mathematical design—he indicates there are seven pieces of armour. However only six are actually mentioned outright.

Jesus called Himself a paraclete, according to John. And He called the Holy Spirit *another* paraclete.

What word did he originally use in Aramaic? I suspect it was from *nasa'* and meant *armour-bearer*. Paraclete itself does not convey the fullness of an armour-bearer, though it comes close.

'Advocate' is an adequate translation of it, but not—in my view—the best. It fails to convey the warrior aspect. But that doesn't mean I would translate *paraclete* as 'armour-bearer' either—simply because we no longer have any sense of what that truly meant.

I think a good translation of *paraclete* which retains both legal and warrior overtones but also harks back to the concept of the armour-bearer is *covenant defender*.

Jesus is the covenant defender of those who belong to Him. So is the Holy Spirit. Marriage partners are called into the covenant defence of each other. This is the true nature of submission: covenant defence.

Right at this moment, we've passed into true danger.

So let's take a check.

All these warfare analogies and these hints about the battle companion or covenant defender—correct as I believe them to be—will almost certainly give us a totally wrong impression of an armour-bearer's nature.

It's such a complex weaving of ideas that the warp and the woof are unimaginably different to the modern mind. But I hope you come to expect the unexpected when it comes to Hebrew thinking. Where else would putting on armour be equated with lifting up?

2

'We have lift-off.'

A THOUSAND YEARS OR SO after the battle at Michmash when Jonathan and his armour-bearer lifted up a new standard for faith, another conflict took place. It was a very personal one for another man called Saul who, like his kingly namesake, was descended from the tribe of Benjamin.

It's early morning. Frost is in the air. Saul stands at the door of his tent—a tent he himself has made. He pulls his woollen tallit around him as he tries to pray. But his thoughts are disturbed, his mind pre-occupied.

He lifts his eyes to the north-west horizon. An eagle soars near snow-clad Mount Hermon, its peak dazzling white in the dawnlight. The Sidonians, he remembers, call it Sirion, the *breastplate*. From this distance it is obvious why. It's a glittering shield of ice.

Its oldest Hebrew name is Sion, *lifted up*, from nasa' through n'siyón.[16]

Lifted up.

Saul lifts his hands in prayer. His thoughts spiral like the eagle, plummeting down to lift from his memory details of the mountain's history.

Sion sounds like—but is very different in meaning to—Zion, *parched*. Throughout the centuries the similarity in the names exerted an almost irresistible pull on the Psalmists. They sang often of Sion and Zion as a unity—north and south meeting in beauty and holiness. True brotherhood, their poetry proclaimed, is as if the dew of Hermon falls like anointing oil on the high priest in the temple in Jerusalem.

Saul sighs at the picture of true brotherhood. How achingly beautiful—as lovely, in fact, as the feet treading the mountains to bring good news—but how impossibly idealistic!

Even the pristine whiteness of the mountain is not a comfort; not now a poetic mood has overtaken him. Its frosty ice-covered slopes remind him that frost, *kaphowr*, is symbolic of atonement. The purity of its whiteness and the derivation of its name from *kaphar*, to cover, contribute to the imagery—helped, mind you, by the fact *kaphar* also means *to make atonement, to reconcile.*

The mountain's broad expanse is a figure of *kapporeth*, the mercy-seat of God, the place of atonement. *At–one–ment*: being at one—the very nature of true brotherhood. His mind is drawn inexorably to the disaster following Yom Kippur, the Day of Atonement.

Each year the High Priest, having made the sacrifice on Yom Kippur, would place a thread of scarlet wool outside the Holy of Holies. It was a hallowed tradition. In three days, the thread would turn snow-white.

Though your sins are like scarlet, they shall be as white as snow. Though they are red like crimson, they shall be as wool. So it was written in the scroll of the prophet Isaiah.[17] The blood-red thread that turned snow–white symbolised God's acceptance of the High Priest's sacrifice for the sin of all the people.

But this year the thread remained red.

How could it not turn white? It was a natural phenomenon, attested since the time of David who prophesied: *My God, my God, why have You forsaken me? ...I am a worm and not a man...*[18]

His words were undoubtedly an allusion to the *cermes vermilio*, the worm that gave its life for its children. In doing so, it created a crimson stain which turned to a white flake in three days.

Other white flakes drift into Paul's mind: snow, manna. All are symbolic of hope and reconciliation. The scarlet thread of Yom

Kippur weaves together the prophecies of David and Isaiah and subtly alludes to God's providence in the time of Moses.

Yet this year the symbol backfired spectacularly.

When the thread had so visibly and publicly remained red, many worshippers were perplexed at God's refusal to accept the sacrifice. They looked to the High Priest and wondered. Some whispered that the followers of The Way were right: the Messiah has come and the need for the sacrifices of bulls or goats is gone.

Yet, if the Messiah has truly come and been raised from the dead, as they say, where is he? All this babble of an empty tomb! But if he's really alive, why isn't he leading the army against the Romans? Why hasn't he swept them into the sea?

The Messiah would re-create the true brotherhood symbolised by Sion and Zion. We, his people, would lift him to greatness and he would be lifted up: his very name would be a banner to draw us all to him.

He would be our armour-bearer. And we, his.

Saul grits his teeth and blows a white plume into the cold air. Hermon is a shield, a breastplate and a helmet—deservedly his anointed symbol.

Saul looks around, realising a preternatural quietness has descended. The usual early morning tinkle of movement from his companions has vanished.

Silence. Not even a muffled echo.

He strains his ears. Nothing. He lowers his hands.

The sparkling shimmer off Sion's slopes has formed a dazzling cloud, shaped like a man's hand. It appears to be coming his way. It's blinding.

Saul blinks.

Still there is no sound in this suddenly eerie place.

He decides to leave. If we go right now, he thinks, we can reach Damascus by afternoon.

But it is already too late. The hand of light descends like a dove...

'So then, Saul, why do you persecute Me?'

One man in a thousand, Solomon says.
Will stick more close than a brother...
...The Thousandth Man will stand your friend
With the whole round world against you.

Rudyard Kipling,
The Thousandth Man

This imaginative reconstruction of the lead-up to Saul's conversion is built around the imagery of an armour-bearer. The concept of divine armour is a theme that recurs in Paul's writings and is of such significance I suspect it was involved with a watershed moment in his thinking—and how much more watershed can you get than his Damascus road experience?

Now I may be mistaken, but I think this is still a valuable exercise in developing a Hebrew mindset.

We don't know where exactly Paul was on the Damascus road when he was smitten by the Light. However it's reasonable to assume it was not too far from his destination and Mount Hermon was likely to be a prominent feature of the landscape.

The highest peak in Israel, Hermon was the absolute essence of oneness in Hebrew thinking. It was an archetypal symbol for it in the Psalms.

How good and pleasant it is when brothers live together in unity!
It is like precious oil poured on the head, running down on the beard,
running down on Aaron's beard, down upon the collar of his robes.

It is as if the dew of Hermon were falling on Mount Zion.
For there the Lord bestows his blessing, even life forevermore.

Psalm 133 NIV

Geographically, it's impossible for the dew of Hermon to fall on Mount Zion.[19] It's in the far north of Israel while Zion is much further south. But the psalmist envisages the landscape folding up, perhaps like a scroll, perhaps like a pleat, so that north and south become as one.

He makes reference to oneness as a sweet anointing, akin to oil so thick and luxurious it flows down the High Priest's beard and onto his clothing. For the Jews, oneness came by covenant.

In various situations, individuals might take out a covenant and become blood brothers—one of these instances was taking up the role of an armour-bearer. As we've seen, it was not 'Gun for Hire'. It was a life commitment.

Paul is unlikely to have known at this point Mount Hermon is the probable site of Jesus' transfiguration but he would have known it had several names which evoke armour.

The Sidonians called it Sirion, *breastplate*. As a breastplate covers the body, so the shimmering snowfields covered the three-peaked mountain.

The Amorites called it Senir or Shenir, *snow mountain*. The word is related to the Hebrew, *tsinnah*, meaning *coldness of snow* and also meaning *shield*.[20]

The oldest Hebrew name for it was Sion from *nasa'*, *to lift up*. And *nasa'* was related to armour-bearer, *the one who lifted up*. The word for armour-bearer, as mentioned previously, also had the sense of *one who protects the head*. Just as a helmet does. So although it didn't mean *helmet*, it had that resonance about it.

The Hebrew word for *banner* was *nissi*, directly derived from *nasa'*. It was one of the names of God: Jehovah Nissi, the lord my banner—*the one who lifts up*. But the overriding message of the story of Moses lifting up his hands during the battle is this: the armour-bearing nature of Jehovah Nissi is mutuality.

That is something we have to write into our hearts. God will lift us up as we lift Him up. Mutual lifting is the essential heart of this divine name.

Oneness of purpose is embodied in it too; the whole idea of being a team, and at one with each other, naturally had its source in being at one with God.

The English word, *atonement*, really does derive from *at–one–ment*: the state of being at one. Although the Bible does not relate the story of the symbolic scarlet thread, the Jewish historian Josephus makes mention of it. Would Paul have known the scarlet thread did not turn white? It appears to have been public knowledge, so it's quite likely.

What he wouldn't have known at this point was that, although the Temple would remain for another thirty-eight years and the Temple sacrifices continue all that time, the scarlet thread would never turn white again.

While we cannot be certain that the crimson dye of the *cermes vermilio* worm was used, it seems the likely explanation for the phenomenon. The Hebrew word for worm, *tolah,* also means *scarlet*. In Bible translations, *tolah* is sometimes rendered *worm,* sometimes *scarlet* and sometimes *crimson*.

A vermillion dye was made from the *cermes vermilio*. This worm sucks the sap of twigs by piercing their thin bark. This enables it to prepare a waxy scale which not only contains the red dye but protects its soft body. The female worm climbs a tree to bear her eggs; the larvae hatch and feed on her body. She gives her life for her children and, in doing so, a crimson stain is left on the tree. When this dries over three days, it changes to white and flakes off.

Jesus' next-to-last words on the cross were from the beginning of Psalm 22. Perhaps those who heard Him were supposed to think of the following words about the worm: the one who gave her life for her children, the one who symbolised atonement and forgiveness of sin, the one who was transformed in three days...

In the twentieth century, sometimes the catch-cry was heard: 'No more worm theology.' We cringed at that kind of put-down and relegated it to the past.

However such symbolism is not a put-down. The worm is not low-life. It is a lofty symbol of forgiveness and restoration.

Forgiveness is sometimes the translation of *nasa'* in Scripture. That's because sins were lifted off and borne away, so *nasa', lift off*, is eminently appropriate.

Nissi, the *banner* or *that which is lifted up*, is related to the modern Hebrew word, *nissu'in, marriage*.

Like *nasu, married*, it tells that old, old story Paul was clearly thinking of when he spoke of submission: marriage is mutual armour-bearing. It is the submission that lifts up, so then the Lord's name may be lifted up.

I walk, I lift up, I lift up heart, eyes,
Down all that glory in the heavens to glean our Saviour;
And, éyes, heárt, what looks, what lips yet gave you a
Rapturous love's greeting of realer, of rounder replies?

Gerard Manley Hopkins, *Hurrahing in Harvest*

I was grossly unfair to Paul in the last chapter, when I suggested he should have consulted his fellow-apostles about the use of words to translate *armour-bearer*. He did indeed use the concept of the paraclete.

At the beginning of the second chapter of his letter to the Philippians, he wrote: *if then there is any encouragement in Christ... make my joy complete: be of the same mind, having the same love, being in full accord and of one mind.*[21]

George Cladis points out that Paul chose to use the word *paraclesis* in this passage, and this is generally translated *encouragement*. Like John Sandford, Cladis also describes the related term 'paraclete' as stemming from military vocabulary.

He reminds us Greek soldiers worked in pairs and that, by standing back-to-back, they covered each other in battle. Cladis describes the paraclete as a 'wingman'.

Isn't that an extraordinary image of the Holy Spirit? A wingman.

Isn't it an amazing picture of Jesus, the first paraclete? The commander of the armies of God is our personal wingman. He is there to cover our backs, to protect us, to call forth our best efforts, to build up our courage, to en*courage* us.

However, it's not simply that Jesus is our paraclete. It is also his call to action. It is the way He expects us to behave with others.

Sure, as George Cladis points out, there are people who make us stumble, sabotage our efforts, block our advance. And sometimes when we meet the enemy, he is us.

But Paul says to us: be like Christ, be of good courage, fortify others with courage and en*courage* one another, be the wingman for others, be their armour-bearer.

Love one another.

Serve one another.

Stand by one another.

This is how we follow Jesus' example and become a paraclete.

A friend loves at all times, and a brother is born for adversity.

Proverbs 17:17 NIV

'Look at the birds in the sky!' said Jesus one day, talking to a crowd about the important things of life and explaining why worrying is a waste of time.[22] I'd like to think that, at the time, He was pointing at some geese.

Geese fly in their characteristic arrowhead formation for a good reason: a lone migrating goose cannot travel nearly the distance the wedge[23] can.

When one bird flaps its wings during flight, the air movement it creates provides an aerodynamic uplift for the goose flying behind. The effort the bird in the rear needs to put in to keep up is less. The young, the weak, the old are all advantaged by the flight formation. Working together, the range the wedge can cover increases 71 percent.

The wedge accomplishes what individual birds could never accomplish separately.

All because of uplift.

Geese get the 'wingman' principle far better than we humans do. Birdbrains as they are, they've got more idea of what armour-bearing means than many people have. It's not just about the practical advantages of uplift in flight. Yes, geese know all about commitment too.

A gardener once clipped the flight feathers of a goose, so it was unable to fly.

When the time came for migration, it struggled to rise into the air. Other geese, seeing it was in trouble, came flapping around. Some had already taken off but they returned. Soon it became clear the goose with the clipped feathers would not be able to make it successfully into the air. The gaggle surrounded it protectively, abandoned their migration and settled back down on a pond to keep it company.

Some weeks later, when the hapless goose's flight feathers had re-grown, they all took off together.

Geese demonstrate their 'till death us do part' commitment to each other in other ways as well. When a bird is too old, infirm or injured to continue the migration, it will begin to lag and lose altitude. As it drops out, unable to keep abreast of the formation, two stronger geese will leave and begin to fly alongside it. Together, they'll find a sheltered location near a pond or stream and settle down, providing food and protection for the bird in need until it recovers. Then they'll all join another formation and head off.

If it dies, the two stronger birds will stay until the end, providing ongoing comfort and nurture. Life is 'on hold' as far as they are concerned, just to care for another goose!

If this is what it means to be a 'silly goose', count me in! Sure it's a 'dog eat dog' world where 'nature is red in tooth and claw'. But it's also a world where self-sacrifice is instinctive, beautiful and under-rated.

I have to suspect that the honk of a goose is a close relation to the language of heaven and that these birdbrains have more true intelligence than many of the best thinkers of our century.

Most of us are unaware our culture actually trains our minds to be attuned to a Greek mould with its distinctive form of logic. This kind of thinking baulks at paradox and finds the patterns of Hebrew block thinking to be almost alien.

Despite our conditioning to hold otherwise, there is nothing innately superior about logic. This is obvious by its ability to recognise paradox but its failure to encompass it. The differences between such modes of thinking create unique challenges of translation. The translator's assumptions play a huge part in it all, as well.

I once failed a translation test because I neglected to specify the exact kind of light Einstein was talking about in a paper on photo-electricity—the examiner saw it as critically important the German word for *diffuse* light had been used. As a physics student translating for a scientific audience, I wasn't convinced it mattered at all. To my way of thinking, the type of light was, in the context of the whole paper, quite irrelevant.

It's said the Eskimo have 19 words for *snow*. The occasions when a reader needs to know the difference between the kinds are few and far between—though, of course, it's another matter entirely for an Arctic explorer.

The author's intentions play a role but the translator's audience may impact the choice of words too.

Psalm 29:9 presents an intriguing problem in translation. The New American Standard Bible renders it: *'The voice of the Lord makes the deer to calve.'* However, the New International Version offers this alternative: *'The voice of the Lord twists the oaks.'*

Deer giving birth and oak trees writhing aren't exactly equivalent concepts—our automatic reaction is to suspect the accuracy of one translation, if not both. However as Jeff Benner points out, the Hebrew word אילה (ayalah) can mean either *deer* or *oaks*.

אילה (ayalah) is the feminine form of איל (ayil) which is *oak, post, ram* or *mighty man*, depending on the context. How can one word mean such dissimilar things?

Abraham offers up איל (ayil), instead of Isaac.[24]

- The angel in Ezekiel's vision measured איל (ayil) in the vestibule of the temple.[25]
- The Lord tells Isaiah that the people will be ashamed of איל (ayil) and the gardens in which they delighted.[26]
- The איל (ayil) of Moab will tremble when they hear how the Lord has delivered His people out of Egypt.[27]
- Essentially what איל (ayil) comes down to is *strong leader.* The

sturdy oak is often considered the finest of trees, the ram is the powerful leader of the flock, just as mighty men are foremost amongst the people, while a pillar in the forecourt of the temple is a post of primary significance. The equivalence of oak, post, ram and mighty man in ancient thinking thus all boils down to their function as *strong leaders*.

This concept of *strong leader* also accounts for the exquisitely evocative name of the morning star in Hebrew. The 'gazelle of dawn' is the brilliant precursor to sunrise, the herald of day: 'ayelet hashachar from ayalah, *deer*.

We simply don't think like this.

We've got neat little boxes and tidy categories and we've been trained to make fine distinctions. So a ram as the functional equivalent of an oak or the morning star really isn't a way of conceptualising that sits easily with us.

We're not Hebrew thinkers, we're Greek thinkers. The Greek legacy of scientific rationalism is integral to our culture and is part of a long tradition of education in the west.

But it wasn't always so.

Our ever widening number of subject specialities, each with its fine narrow focus, leads to fragmentary information, not integrated wisdom.

I've written at length about names, their effects and the choices inherent in them in the first book in this series, *God's Poetry*. The power of our own names to call us into our destiny or to cut us off from it is rarely appreciated.

In some African tribes, it's said that when a child is born, the father takes the baby away into the silence of the bush. He cradles the new-born against his chest. He holds it close, listening to the drumming of its heartbeat, the harmony of its breathing, its rhythm of life. His spirit reaches out to commune with that of the baby. Some hours might go by before he can be sure of the child's true name but, when he is, he whispers that secret in its ear.

For the next thirteen years or so, the child will not be known by that name but by another instead: something as common as Johnny or Billy. But then at the right time, when he is initiated into the tribe, his secret name will be revealed and its power unleashed along with it.

Craig Hill of *Ancient Paths* (now *Family Foundations*) says that when a Hebrew boy reached the same age and was ready for his bar mitzvah—the ceremony where he would become a *son of the covenant*—his father would lift him high on his shoulders and run around the village in celebration, shouting to the cheers of uncles and cousins: 'This is my beloved son, in whom I am well-pleased.'

I don't know if this is true but it makes sense. When the Holy Spirit alighted on Jesus as a dove during His baptism in the Jordan and a voice was heard from Heaven, this was the moment of His personal call into the ancient covenant of the people of Israel. But it was also the moment when His true identity was finally revealed.

For the African tribesman, the name the father whispered in a child's ear was his true identity, not to be revealed until the right moment.

The Hebrews had a similar belief about true identity but took it a step further back. Life itself was imparted when God breathed into a soul by giving to it a part of His own name.[28] When the Father whispered in the unborn's ear, He spoke of identity and purpose as He passed on the wellspring of life itself. When God breathed life into Adam, the word used is not the well-known *ruach* but instead the incredibly evocative *nashamah*.[29]

Yes, the first word related to human *breathing* in the Bible is not derived from *ruach,* spirit, but instead from *nashamah* for *breath.*

And the Lord God formed man[30] *of the dust of the ground*[31]*, and* *breathed into his nostrils the breath* [nashamah] *of life; and man became a living soul* [nephesh].

Genesis 2:7

The words for *breath* and *soul* are intimately related—*nashamah* produces *nephesh*, because it is the breath of the Lord which gives life to humanity. The central letters of *nashamah* are *shem* which means *name*. It is for this reason that the rabbis taught that God breathed life into our souls through naming.

Throughout the ancient world, naming was a sacred act. It was the word by which a child was called into his calling. It was the voice of destiny, summoning the child into his future with all its glorious promise.

When God cut a covenant with Abram (*and* Sarai, as will be obvious in a moment), part of that ceremony was the name exchange. Abram and Sarai become Abraham and Sarah: each receiving within their names a significant 'H'. This is an abbreviation for HaShem, *the name*, itself an abbreviation for *the name of God*.

In the modern world we treat names like labels, even if we believe they are profoundly more. We fail to understand the nature of the covenants governing them; we're generally blind to the fact that covenants—with one notable exception—are forever and involve generations within a family; and we have absolutely no knowledge of the power of names to bind us, as prisoners, so we are locked out of our destinies instead of ushered into them.

Names are power.

They are the power to form identity; they are the power that calls upon us to enter our destiny and they are the power to breathe life itself into us. Hating your own name has radical consequences. If you do, it may be time to sit with the Father until you find out what name He gave you when, like that African tribesman, He held you close to His heart.

When Jesus was asked to bless some children, He didn't just

pat their heads as was the common custom of rabbis at the time. The Greek text indicates these were infants and He cradled them, enfolding them and lingering over the moment as he blessed them individually and spoke intentionally into their lives. He took so long He started to annoy some people.

A true blessing calls you into the destiny God has prepared for you before the foundation of the world, so I have to suspect Jesus was whispering the children's true names to them. Or, if not their true names, at least the truth about their names—and about His.

It is only when Jesus instituted the new covenant in His blood that He also first gave instructions for His followers to approach the Father in His name.[32] Prayers in Jesus' name are only possible because of the name covenant He instituted.

Most Westerners today have no idea legally-binding spiritual covenants may already exist over their own names. By their nature, covenants are everlasting and follow family lines. Moreover they are rarely with the triune God who created the cosmos. They are often a fatal and syncretistic mix of spiritualities.

Names, let alone name covenants, are powers we hardly ever take seriously. We've bought into the modern concept that most names are spiritually neutral and their meaning can be summed up in one or two words: we do not grasp the idea that the names God has breathed into us, the wellspring of our souls, are poems.

It's that Greek rationalist mechanistic thinking again! Focussing in on one tiny aspect rather than stepping back to survey the big picture.

Our names are poetic symphonies, not the single musical note most books suggest.

Unless they are harmonies of light, not discordant noises in the darkness, we need to be proactive about working through, with fear and trembling, that part of our identity which so often speaks of a different Lord than Jesus of Nazareth.[33]

Oh, that He would smother me with His kisses—the very Spirit-kiss of His mouth.*

*This Spirit-kiss is what made Adam, the man of clay, into a living expression of God. Dust and Deity meet as the Maker kissed His Spirit wind into Adam. The Word of God is the Kiss from the mouth of our Beloved, breathing upon us the revelation of His love.

Songs of Songs 1:2 TPT

If this interpretation of nashamah by the rabbis is right, and I think it is, then it is naming that creates soul. When God names us, we are given life. But as I look at nashamah, *breath*, and neshama, *soul*, with their embedded letters shem, *name*, I notice something even more obvious. The words for *breath* and *soul* begin with the same letters as nasa'.

If we go back to the basic meaning of נשא —nasa' or nasah— it is essentially *lift up* or *lift off*.

Ahh! So here's the secret of life: it's a complex interweaving of lifting up, naming and breathing all within God's presence.

Perhaps this is why many non-Christian religions have breathing exercises which invoke an idol's name or title. The enemy of our soul never comes up with a new trick, instead he always tries to counterfeit the works of our Creator Father.

However nasa' does not only mean *lift up*. It can also be translated as, among others: *to carry, carry away, carry off, take, accept, assist, bear, bear away, bring, ease, endure, forgive, ever forgive, forgiven, exalt, lofty, married, rise, raise, shield-bearer, shield-carrier, armour-bearer, support, sustain, pardon.*

God's Panoply

Look at these meanings! Jesus must have used this word in every other sentence. As He talked about bearing one another's burdens, forgiving each other, His yoke being easy, the Son of Man being lifted up, carrying our cross, being humbled or exalted, the sending of another paraclete.

As we look back on the story of Jonathan and his paraclete—his armour-bearer—we have a picture of what our own relationship with Jesus should be. Imagine Jesus, the divine armour-bearer, saying to you, 'Do whatever is in your heart!' Imagine the Holy Spirit, the paraclete, saying, 'I am with you soul and mind.'

Yet as we put on the armour of God and submit to become an armour-bearer ourselves, that's exactly what happens. Bearing one another's burdens, forgiving each other, supporting each other in friendship and love, lifting up and carrying each other through the heat of battle: such ideas aren't so incompatible after all, are they, when we start to move into Hebrew thinking?

Nasa' is such an important word, it's worth committing to memory and adding to your permanent vocabulary.

Here's an easy way to remember it.

NASA in the modern world is an acronym for the National Aeronautic and Space Administration: the body of scientists, engineers and technicians responsible for the US Space programme. 'We have lift-off,' was the catch-phrase announced as each massive rocket successfully rose into the air.

So think a **NASA** rocket as it leaves the launch pad: think '*We have lift-off*.'

Isn't it remarkable that over three thousand years after Jonathan and his armour-bearer climbed the cliffs of Michmash, the word still has the same connotations, even across a massive language barrier? It's utterly awesome such a significant word should survive the ravages of time and transcend cultures in such a beautiful and uplifting way.

...with silent lifting mind I've trod
The high, untrespassed sanctity of space,
Put out my hand and touched the face of God.

John Gillespie Magee Jnr, *High Flight*

3

Just, not fair

IN 1835, THE BIBLE SOCIETY published 100 copies of the Gospel of Luke in the Māori language. The following year, missionaries gave one of these to Tarore, a Māori girl at a mission school near Matamata. She treasured it and read it to her father Ngākuku, the chief of the Waikato tribe. When she slept, she kept it under her pillow.

On October 19, 1836, a raiding party from the Rotorua tribe killed Tarore.

Her treasure was stolen and given to Te Uira, the chief of the Rotorua tribe. He was unable to read, so it was ripped apart for cartridges.

One day, however, a slave named Ripahau who had just been freed came that way on his journey home. He was literate and, realising what the remaining pages were, read them to the Rotorua chief.

Deeply moved by what he heard, Te Uira resolved to seek out Tarore's father and beg for forgiveness.

But this was the land of *utu*, payback.

Ngākuku would only be keeping ancestral tradition if he took the opportunity to avenge himself on his daughter's killer. The risk Te Uira took in going to him was unthinkable.

Yet forgiveness prevailed. Peace was established between tribes that had been at war for generations.

The story of the two chiefs who had been brought together by Tarore and her copy of the Gospel of Luke was so extraordinary it spread almost as fast as the wildfire that killed off the moa. It was a living example of reconciliation, rather than revenge. And it was such a profound testimony to the power of forgiveness that, as missionaries penetrated further into New Zealand, they discovered many Māori tribes waiting for them. Already converted as a result of the story, they wanted to know more about a way of life free of revenge.

Only mercy is more important than justice and only justice is more important than mercy.

Anne Hamilton

One of the meanings of nasa' is forgiveness.[34] There's an odd thing about forgiveness many people don't quite grasp: it follows that same law of mutuality Moses discovered during the battle with the Amalekites. Jesus expresses this mutuality in part of his most famous prayer: *Forgive us our sins as we forgive those who sin against us.*

Many people experience a sense of something being lifted off them when they forgive someone who has wounded them. Often people say they feel so much 'lighter'. And of course, this is natural, because as we lift off our judgments of others, those same judgments are divinely lifted from us.

We are judged with the measure with which we judge.

It's a legal universe. Despite the anathema with which modern

Christianity tends to approach the Law of God, these legal aspects are very fortunate. Both physically and spiritually.

Imagine the chaos if gravity were a capricious force. What if electromagnetism decided to have a day off occasionally? What if, to every action, there was—not an equal and opposite reaction—but an arbitrary unknown response? You could slam the brakes and find yourself accelerating.

If chemical equations balanced only when they felt like it, the pharmaceutical industry could not exist. How could we create medicines, fuel for our cars or even dinner recipes?

I first began to appreciate the importance of stability in law back when I was in junior high school. My history teacher had given the class an assignment on 'totalitarianism'. I'd just started in on it when I happened to encounter the husband of one of my mum's friends. He was from Poland and had been in a Nazi concentration camp during the Second World War. He feared to return to his homeland in case he was executed by the Soviet secret police. His hatred of both Germans and Russians was immense.

He asked those safe questions adults always fall back on when they don't know how to converse with a kid: *How's school? What have you got for homework?* As I told him, I decided to seek his opinion on one of the harder aspects of the assignment: 'Would you say that it's better to be without law than to endure a totalitarian system like Stalinist Russia?'

Intense grey eyes suddenly bored into me. His answer was one I have never forgotten: '*Any* system of law, no matter how brutal, repressive or tyrannical, is better than none. When I was in the concentration camp, nothing, absolutely nothing, compared to the barbarity of the time between the Nazis leaving and the Russians arriving. *Any* system of law is better than anarchy.'

As I've recalled this statement over the years, I've realised it contains the essence of a truth Christians have largely forgotten. *Law is an aspect of God's grace.*

According to Vishal Mangalwadi, until the eighteenth century, Christians took this as self-evident. The gift of the Ten Commandments freed mankind from anarchy and lawlessness.

Yet human nature tends to inveterate law-breaking: so we desire mercy, not justice. By the nineteenth century, mercy was seen to embody God's grace while justice was not.

Greek thinking, you may recall, is uncomfortable with paradox. So as the Enlightenment progressed, rationalism pushed towards the elimination of concepts perceived as illogical. It did this in all spheres of knowledge. Christians followed along and the heavenly tension they perceived was soon resolved. Most people decided to excise justice from their thinking when it came to the character of God, but to retain mercy.

Medieval people would have said they exiled one of the Four Daughters of God: the redoubtable Lady Justice. There have been times in history when one of the other members of the sisterhood—Justice, Mercy, Truth and Peace—was banished but this was the age when Lady Justice took her turn.

Of course, there were understandable reasons why nineteenth century people did this. The notorious judges who sentenced children to hard labour or transportation for stealing bread were excessive in their zeal for law.

However as the twentieth century approached, this general trend resulted in a theology which separated law from grace. According to Mangalwadi, around this time Christian colleges started to drop their law departments. Those retaining them became increasingly secularised. This wholesale departure of Christians from legal studies has had enormous consequences for law-making within the twenty-first century.

The fact is that when we separate law and grace—and make grace more important—it's natural to consider law passé. We may not become completely lawless, we may not think ourselves above the law, but we certainly begin to act as if we're entitled to forgiveness.

So much so that we're apt to accuse others of being unchristian even when we deliberately hurt them, make a conscious decision to do wrong or intentionally fail to do what is right. The best form of defence being a good offence, we've created the ultimate sin: judgmentalism.

Forgiveness is no longer an aspect of God's character, but a god in its own right.

Once the sisterhood of the Four Daughters of God was broken up and Lady Justice cast out, it didn't take long for grace to become tawdry. Before the middle of the twentieth century, Dietrich Bonhoeffer—martyred during the Second World War—was talking of 'cheap grace'.

Grace is not given that we might continue to sin. No one is entitled to grace: that is a denial of its character. To automatically count on forgiveness as a right and not an unexpected gift and undeserved privilege is ultimately to repudiate all Four Daughters of God.

Truth degenerates in a world where forgiveness creates a licence for everything from mild misbehaviour to serious crime. It becomes relative.

If Peace is constantly raped and violated, but has to keep on forgiving without any hope of Justice, then who will keep the peace?

Unless we revive the heavenly tension of justice and mercy, we demean both. Instead of teetering between one extreme and another, we need a return to the ancient block thinking that embraces both.

...children are innocent and love justice, while most of us are wicked and naturally prefer mercy.

GK Chesterton

The law of Christ.

Jesus—the grace-giver, the essence and epitome of a love that transcends justice—gave us a law.

Bear one another's burdens.

He gave us a commandment too: *Love one another as I have loved you.*

Mutuality, again.

Both the law and the command express God's grace and also summarise every law and command He has ever given.

Bear one another's burdens is another concept stemming from the root word nasa'. And yet another petal on the same flower is forgiveness.

What is forgiveness? I was very surprised to find that I didn't know. I was even more surprised by the way I discovered that I didn't know.

It was when I was writing my first novel: the scene about forgiveness took an unexpected turn. Instead of a commendation for her tolerant attitude, the heroine was chastised for never forgiving anyone. My fingers typed the words, failing to follow the instructions of my head.

Although I had not intended to write the words I did, I also felt they were mysteriously right. 'Why does Holly never forgive anyone?' I asked the book in perplexity. 'Because,' it answered, 'she excuses their behaviour, finding reasons for their actions in their upbringing or their ignorance. She rationalises her excuses as pardon.'

You may think that books don't talk to their authors but, if you are 'serving the work' properly in the way Madeleine L'Engle suggests, you should discover truth about yourself in what you write.[35] In fact, any author who isn't interrogating their own work to find out what is truly in their heart is not taking advantage of the gift God gives them through their writing.

So I realised as I finished the scene between Holly and Ruēl that I avoided forgiveness in exactly the same way she did. I excused; I didn't forgive.

I've found many people like I used to be. Some of them actually cannot see that there is any difference between excusing and forgiving. For them, to understand is to forgive.

In fact, to understand is simply to understand. It may pave the way for forgiveness but it is not forgiveness itself.

Forgiveness is *not* equivalent to mercy: that's a common mistake in people's thinking. Rather, it is a combination of justice and mercy. Excusing gives the illusion of forgiveness while cleverly sidestepping it by removing justice from the equation.

Justice of course requires a judgment—a ruling on the basis of natural law to establish the severity of the offence. (By natural law, I mean that innate sense of fairness we're all born with; not the judicial system of precedent and technicality which only accidentally and occasionally has an intersection with anything like true justice.[36]) Without that judgment, the dignity and worth of the victim is trivialised. Even dismissed.

In *The Sunflower*, Simon Wiesenthal told of a dilemma he faced one day during World War II. A Jew, he was taken to see a dying SS officer. The young soldier, swathed in bandages, struggling for breath, spoke of an atrocity he'd been forced to participate in. It was tormenting his conscience so deeply he'd asked for a Jew to be brought to him in order to ask for forgiveness.

Eventually Wiesenthal turned away and left the room without a word. Later he spoke with others of what he did and what he should have done. Almost overwhelmingly, Jewish people agree with his action. Christians urge forgiveness.

Os Guinness, in his foreword to one edition of the story, makes several profound observations about this divide.

Wiesenthal was certainly not hard-hearted. He conceals the identity of the officer though it is clear he knew who he was. He reveals moreover that, in a later encounter with the man's mother, he was careful to preserve her belief that her son died in heroic defence of the Fatherland. In addition, Hitler's friend Albert Speer wrote warmly of God's grace touching him when Wiesenthal spent time with him.

Guinness ascribes the vogue of 'contrition chic'[37] to several factors:

- a non-judgmental vacuous tolerance that promotes the idea it is more evil to judge evil than do it
- a political trend of apologising for the sins committed by our ancestors in the distant past, but not our own
- a shift in importance from 'character' to 'image' which reduces confession to a plea bargain, a calculated step in the public rehabilitation process

Ultimately, as Guinness points out 'cheap-grace forgiveness is a powerful collusion in appeasing evil'.[38]

A forgiveness that does not count the cost is not forgiveness at all.

Because the heart is deceitful above all things, as well as the wellspring of life, it has devised many clever ways of avoiding forgiveness.[39] It:

- excuses and tolerates
- understands and rationalises
- even denies the existence of evil and sin—thereby trivialising abuse and harm while trying to do precisely the opposite

There was a woman who realised the line in the Lord's Prayer 'forgive us as we forgive' was actually asking for trouble. After some time, she resolved the problem she had with it—not by forgiving others but simply by not praying those particular words anymore.

It's just not fair!

It's just, not fair!

What a difference a comma makes.

For twenty years I coordinated an annual camp for primary school children based around the *Chronicles of Narnia* by CS Lewis. As time went by, the leadership chose the motto, *It's just, not fair!* as the camp's watchword. We began to experiment with the structure of the teams, realising that it's not fair to treat individuals equally but it's not fair to treat them unequally either. As I look back, we were struggling with the realisation that equal treatment does not recognise individuality and therefore is not true justice.

We did things that would be impossible in the current post-post-modern climate. We'd have a team of two, a team of eight and a team of ten. By the end of the first day, the team of two would be so far behind in the points score, they knew it would take a miracle for them to catch up. 'Why?' they'd ask. 'Why are there only two of us? We can never win.'

'Life isn't about winning,' we'd say. 'We're teaching you a very valuable lesson: life's *not* fair.'

By the end of the second day when the other teams were ten thousand points ahead, that life lesson had worn pretty thin for the two-kid team. They were pretty close to despair and had all but given up trying to compete.

Then we'd hold the Narnian Olympics. One of the first games was *Pass the Orange*. The teams would have to send an orange down the entire length of their team and back again, using only their necks. No hands allowed!

The eight and ten-member teams would rise up in indignation and outrage as they realised how easy it would be for the two-kid team to win 5000 points. 'It's not fair!' they'd scream.

I'd raise my eyebrows and turn to the two boys who were 10000 points behind. 'Gentlemen, I don't know how it could possibly have happened but these people seem to have missed out on the message you've been learning for the last two days. They've had it easy while you've had it tough. Please explain to them in three words the truth about life.'

With smiles suddenly as wide as the Nile delta and as toothsome as crocodiles, they'd turn together and say: 'Life's *not* fair.'

By the end of the Narnian Olympics, the points score would be close to equalised. Afterwards the two boys would sidle up to the leaders on the quiet. 'We stand a chance, don't we?'

'Life's not fair,' we'd say. 'But that's not what we really want you to learn. We want you to realise life's just, not fair. That invisibly, behind the scenes, a God of justice rules. Most people don't see the justice because they give up too soon.'

The boys would nod sagely. 'Don't ever give up,' they'd say as they went off happy.

Year after year, all three teams would end up with exactly the same number of points in the final tally on the last day.

One time one of the campers stared at the chalkboard with the final result, frowning long after everyone else had gone off to pack their things. 'What's up?' I asked him. 'Do you think there's a mistake?'

'No,' he said. 'I was trying to work out how it's done. The last two camps had a three-way tie too.'

'You think we've rigged the result?'

'I can't see how... but...' He searched my face, his eyes narrow with suspicion. '...you're a maths teacher, aren't you?'

I nodded. 'But what'd be the point of rigging it?'

He grinned as he went off. 'Because life's just, not fair?'

The Lord their God will save them in that day... they shall be like the jewels of a crown, lifted like a banner over His land.

Zechariah 9:16 NKJV

I love the fact it's a legal universe, not an anarchic one. I'm especially thankful this is true within the spiritual realms. Anyone who has ever ministered to someone oppressed by evil spirits can celebrate the fact the cosmos is so legal even demons have to obey its laws. Once their legal foothold is removed in a life, they are compelled to leave.

Admittedly, back in the material world, there are times when I find gravity's resemblance to the decrees of the kings of the Medes and the Persians very inconvenient. There are moments I'd like Newton's second law of motion—*To every action there is an equal and opposite reaction*—to cease to exist.

Yet Jesus Himself recognises just such a law operating in heaven when He modelled the 'terrible petition'[40] for us in the Lord's Prayer: *forgive us our sins as we forgive those who sin against us.*

I was particularly adept at not forgiving while thinking I had done so. In taking care not to condemn anyone, I had rationalised their actions by taking into consideration their ignorance or brokenness. So proficient was I at avoiding forgiveness there were times when I even got around it by blaming myself for the hurts and wounds others inflicted on me. I remember one particular instance very vividly: it took me all of four years to wake up and declare with abrupt finality, 'How on earth could I be responsible for what happened? I was never involved in the decision-making process and knew absolutely nothing about it! I'm a hundred percent innocent.' As I reflected on the process by which I took on total blame for this situation and the person in charge had shifted the responsibility to me in such a way I actually came to believe in my own guilt, I became interested in two aspects of it:

- the subtle ways human beings avoid not blame, but forgiveness
- the nature of evil

On the second subject, I recommend the book *Sin: Radical Evil in Soul and Society* by Ted Peters. It really helped me to make judgments while not becoming judgmental, to discern the hallmarks of true evil and to take appropriate, not inappropriate, blame. I hasten to add I don't agree with all of it but it's still the best book I've come across on the topic.

On the matter of forgiveness, I've noticed several things over the course of my life:

- For many people, the hardest person to forgive is the one who is guilty of hurting them or someone they love. They know they haven't forgiven, they're perfectly clear in their own mind. Some of these people want to forgive, others don't; but either way, they aren't deluded about the matter. They don't actually think they *have* forgiven when they *haven't*.

- For some people, the hardest person to forgive is themselves. This is the person who is genuinely guilty, as opposed to someone who has taken on the blame for someone else. They will forgive others but not themselves. Few Christians realise this is an idolatrous position. You've placed yourself higher than the Judge of the Universe. If God has forgiven you, who are you to deny His decree?

- For a few, the hardest person to forgive is the one innocent of all wrongdoing, simply for being innocent. If this seems surprising and almost incomprehensible, remember most people need someone *else* to blame. When the blame for their own actions or those of someone they idolise cannot be projected onto someone else, they actually find it hard to forgive that person for their innocence. To protect their own self-image (or that of the person they idolise), they project blame onto an innocent person.

- And then there are those of us who've mastered the art of tolerance to a degree where we never have to forgive anything. We think that to understand is to forgive but, in fact, it's simply to excuse. We're apt to confuse unconditional love with unconditional acceptance of any misbehaviour, any offence, any evil. I gave up being tolerant when I realised it was being used to manipulate me into accepting the unacceptable. Now I'm civil. Civility requires mutual respect. I don't require people to agree with me or my views but I do require them to respect my right to hold different opinions and a different worldview.

Mutuality: the heart of nasa'. Jehovah Nissi, *the lord my banner*, could not have spelled it out more clearly to Moses and Joshua, Aaron and Hur.

Mutuality: the heart of true forgiveness. Jesus could not have spelled it out more clearly: *forgive as we forgive*.

Mutuality: the heart of covenantal armour-bearing.

His faithful promises are your armour and protection.

Psalm 91: 4 NLT

The influence of Tarore's story on Christianity in Aotearoa was immense. In the Waikato area, where her father Ngākuku was chief, deep change not only took hold but lasted. A quarter of a century later, king Tāwhiao forbade the Māori of the Waikato to retaliate against the violence of British colonialists. His inspirational speech in 1881—'*The killing of men must stop; the destruction of land must stop. I shall bury my patu in the earth and it shall not rise again...*

Waikato, lie down. Do not allow blood to flow from this time on'—
was remembered long beyond his time. Waikato Māori refused to
fight in World War I as a consequence.

The New Zealand government, once jubilant this fierce Māori
tribe had so ardently embraced the ideals of pacifism, was now
angry and embarrassed. In response, they brought in conscription
specifically for the Tainui-Waikato people and exempted other
Māori iwi. The people of Waikato continued to resist. Most of the
conscripts chose to suffer harsh punishments by the military rather
than join the army by force. Throughout the duration of the war, no
Tainui soldiers were sent overseas.

Across the Tasman Strait in Australia, conscription was such a
controversial issue it was put to a nationwide referendum. Even the
most belligerent hawks of war were generally against conscription
and the referendum was defeated.

It was finally brought in—but not until the Vietnam War—and
much of the bitterness surrounding its surprise introduction was
because it had been so thoroughly opposed by ordinary people in
repeated referendums over more than fifty years.

Christianity, as a whole, does not embrace peace gladly. The
Quaker movement is generally overlooked. We're not only a warlike
bunch, we're happy to be that way.

As both a reader and a writer, I love Christian fantasy. However
I am constantly disturbed by the level of violence acceptable
within the genre. No sex, but plenty of gratuitous carnage. I'm
even more alarmed by the recommendations I've received on the
occasions when I have been troubled enough by a book to mention
this concern publicly. Maybe I shouldn't be discreet and keep the
book's title concealed because, invariably and ironically, the list
of recommendations is always topped by the very book that has
caused me to speak out in the first place.

Yet within this culture where violence is normal, we enormously
admire and lionise people like Mahatma Gandhi.

Long before his time, passive resistance was practised in New Zealand by the Māori of Parihaka. *Turn the other cheek, walk the extra mile, love your enemies* became real to these people when in 1880, 1600 soldiers moved against them to confiscate their land. Children went out to greet the soldiers with flowers. The villagers remained seated while the soldiers raided and destroyed their village.

Acts of defiance were perpetrated, but not with guns. By erecting fences and ploughing land.

Hundreds were arrested and jailed, mostly without trial.

The resistance movement of Parihaka, influenced by the teachings of the prophet Te Whiti o Rongomai who was himself influenced by Christianity, was an exemplar of peace, truth, forgiveness and reconciliation.

Blessed are the peacemakers, said Jesus.

Yet so much of Christianity cloaks itself in martial garb and adopts a heavy focus on spiritual warfare, taking down strongholds and re-claiming territory taken by the enemy of our souls.

Paul, after all, directs us on numerous occasions to put on armour to be ready for battle—whether that armour is of light, or of righteousness, or of God or just a piece or two, such as a breastplate and helmet.[41]

Are we meant to understand this armour as designed for attack or defence?

Or was he making a point so different we've entirely missed the significance of what he said? Before we can answer that question, we need to look at what the essence of a covenant is.

4

The Art of Heart-Knitting

THE SEVENFOLD CEREMONY FOR MAKING a blood covenant was rich with symbolism. The ritual of blood brotherhood was not undertaken lightly. Two primary elements were the sacrifice of a goat, bull or lamb and the walk of blood.

The animal was killed and cut in half down the centre. The pieces were placed a distance apart with a pool of blood in the middle.

The participants then walked around the pieces in a figure ∞ (which is now, very appropriately, a symbol of infinity). They stopped in the pool of blood to pronounce both a blessing and a curse.

The curse: if I violate this covenant may I die, just as this animal has died.

The blessing: I will give my life for you if necessary, just as this animal gave its life.

When Jesus made a new covenant in His blood with us, He took this ancient notion a step further. He gave us the blessing but, inveterate covenant-breakers as we are, He did not allow the curses to descend on us. He took them on Himself.

He is both the lamb who was slain and the Good Shepherd who lays down His life for the sheep, including those of a hidden sheepfold.

We're back in the world of Hebrew paradox. He is both the lamb who identifies with us, His fellow-sheep, and the Shepherd who cares for the flock.

Agnus Dei, qui tollis peccata mundi, miserere nobis.

Lamb of God, you who take away the sins of the world, have mercy upon us.

Based on John 1:29

There were three exchanges in a seven-part covenant ceremony:
- the exchange of coats
- the exchange of belts
- the exchange of names

A coat, or mantle, was a symbol of
  - dignity
  - destiny
  - identity
  - authority

By removing their coats and giving them to the other person, the participants confer on each other their own honour and dignity. They exchange destinies and bestow on one another the identity and authority belonging to them as a member of a tribe.

Here is the reason Saul was so angry with Jonathan for cutting a covenant with David. In doing so, Jonathan divested himself of his inheritance—the kingship of Israel—confirming the anointing of Samuel on David.

It also indicates Saul's manipulative streak. He'd simply used the covenant of the armour-bearer to gain his own ends, not to put himself in heart-to-heart relation with his battle-companion.

Because: in effect the exchange of coats says: 'Everything *I am* is yours.'

The second exchange, the exchange of belts, says: 'Everything *I have* is yours.'

In this part of the ceremony the participants would remove the belts holding their weapons. They exchanged them all, including sword, sling and bow. This symbolised their commitment to spend their strength in total defence of each other, should the need arise. The action said, 'Your enemies are now my enemies. If you are attacked, I will come to defend you in the same way as I would defend myself.'

The third exchange was that of names. It says: *'It is no longer "I" who live, but "we".'* As the participants adopted each other's name, they died to themselves as individuals. They became one heart beating in two bodies. A remnant of this part of the ceremony still exists in weddings where the bride takes on her new husband's name.

The tide of time shall never
his covenant remove;
his name shall stand forever,
that name to us is love.

James Montgomery

A name covenant can exist in its own right, though it's now rare for it to do so. The modern-day remnant of such older name covenants is when parents adopt children and call them by their own surnames. The name covenant is just one of the four types of covenant identified by Henry Clay Trumball as pervading the ancient world and still being practised into the late nineteenth century:

- name covenant
- salt covenant
- blood covenant
- threshold covenant

Quite often, the covenants were mixed: the covenant of the armour-bearer, for instance, which we are currently considering, combined the blood covenant, the salt covenant and the name covenant.

A marriage ceremony which includes a wedding cake, a change of name for the bride and in which the groom lifts the bride across the threshold contains faint, barely discernible echoes of the salt covenant, name covenant and threshold covenant.

It's no coincidence that marriage is about a man and a woman becoming one.

It is a very special covenant. Just as the vows of a covenant made by an armour-bearer are so much more than the contract a bodyguard might agree to, so is covenantal marriage vastly much more than a partnership.

Many writers today consider that marriage is a separate covenant in its own right. To the foregoing list they would add:

- marriage covenant
- sandal covenant

The last involves inheritance and is typified by the action of the kinsman-redeemer in the book of Ruth who takes off his sandal and gives it to Boaz, symbolising: *'I give you the right to walk where I would have walked.'*

This makes six types of covenant in total. Is one missing? Seven types would seem far more likely. Or are there too many? Are some of the six mentioned simply just specialised types of another in the list?

The ceremonies for covenants and rites—such as that of the kinsman-redeemer—were so familiar to the early Israelites, the specific details are not given in any one place in Scripture. So it's quite possible that in a blood covenant ceremony, sandals were exchanged at the same time as the mantle. A transfer of inheritance would naturally be enfolded within a transfer of destiny.

On the other hand, we need to be careful to distinguish the essential difference between a contract and a covenant. Not all significant contracts are covenants.

If the sandal transfer[42] was intended to bring the two people involved into oneness, then it is a covenant. However if just a commercial exchange is taking place, merely a transfer of property, then it's a different case. Exchange is *not* the true essence of covenant. The heart of covenant is oneness.

He who by a mother's love made
the wandering world his own
every year comes from above,
comes the parted to atone...
binding earth to the Father's throne.

But thou comest every day,
no, thou never didst depart,
never hour hast been away;
always with us, Lord, thou art...
binding, binding, heart to heart.

George MacDonald

As well as the three exchanges in a covenant ceremony, there were also the cut and the meal. It was the cut—the permanent mark in the flesh—that distinguished the covenant from a simple contract and resulted in the term 'to cut a covenant'.

Using a blade, an incision was made on the palms or the wrists of the participants.

'Behold, I have carved you on the palms of My hands,' said the Lord in Isaiah 49:16, referring to this aspect of the covenant. [43] *'I will never forget you.'*

Once blood was flowing, the participants would shake hands to intermingle it. Sometimes a woollen thread was tied around the clasped hands so, as it was drawn around the wrists, the blood would blend even further. For the Hebrews, the life was in the blood so this represented the deepest possible joining of lives. John Sandford suggests this woollen thread may be considered as the precursor of the traditional wedding ring.

In some cultures and places, wine was used instead of a thread: the blood of the participants dripped into a cup of wine and mingled there. Each then drank from the cup. In other cultures, the union was symbolised in other ways. For instance, according to Henry Clay Trumball, this aspect of the covenant was quite different in India where the spilling of blood was taboo. Instead, the participants would exchange bracelets.

However when there was a 'cut' involved, this part of the ceremony would be finished by rubbing ash or some other substance into the cut so that it would never heal cleanly. A very visible permanent mark would always identify those who had cut a covenant with another.

Lastly, to end the seven parts of a covenant ceremony, there would be a meal. Often this was of bread and wine. Sometimes the wine used to mix the blood would be reserved for this section. Since bread was made with salt, this final ritual was an expression of the everlasting nature of what had transpired between the recipients: a covenant of salt was one that endured forever.

The participants fed each other at this point, symbolising yet again that not only were their hearts one but so were their lives. Their names had been exchanged, their lifeblood had mingled, now each—as symbolised by the food—was being taken totally into the other.

They had come together.

A new relationship had begun, a relationship of love.

But not the sexual love or motherly love or even the love of friends that characterises our impoverished modern notions of 'love'. This is the Greek *agápē* or the Hebrew *chesed*, the latter a difficult word, variously translated *truth, faith, faithful love, faithfulness, loyalty, lovingkindness.*

There's one old-fashioned word that fits these: *troth.*

As in *betrothed.*

As in a love epitomised by the words: 'I will never leave you nor forsake you.'

And characterised by God's words: '*Behold, I have carved you on the palms of My hands.*'

Now Thomas...one of the Twelve, was not with the disciples when Jesus came. So the other disciples told him, 'We have seen the Lord!' But he said to them, 'Unless I see the nail marks in His hands and put my finger where the nails were... I will not believe it.'

John 20:24–25 NIV

The wounds that Jesus bears on His hands are the engraved marks of a covenant. Indeed the very word for the palm of the hand is related to a whole trove of covenant-connected words.

The palm in Hebrew is kaph, *the hollow part of the hand*; it is related to caph, *the hollow basinstone of threshold sacrifice.* It is from kaph that, according to Jeff Benner, the English word *cup* comes.[44]

So too does the name Cephas—the nickname given by Jesus to his disciple Simon the fisherman. In Greek, Cephas was Petros. We render it in English as Peter and give its meaning as *rock* or *stone*.

But that's to miss its immense significance and wealth of undertone. Cephas and, by association, Peter don't just mean a stone, but a cornerstone—for a householder of ancient times this signified the stone underlying the doorway which was the place of 'pass over' and covenant-cutting.

In the temple, the word most closely related to this was the mercy-seat, *kapporeth*.

Now it was in the shadow of Mount Hermon that Jesus gave Simon his new name.

Just a year or two later, it was also in the shadow of Mount Hermon that Paul saw a blinding light and heard a voice from heaven.

In fact, it was on Mount Hermon that Peter himself saw a blinding light and also heard a voice from heaven.

The Sidonians might have called it Sirion, the *breastplate* of ice; the oldest Hebrew name for it might have been Sion, *lifted up*; the Psalmists might have seen it as the ultimate symbol of oneness and brotherhood; but Hermon has a dark aspect to it too. According to the Book of Enoch—a prophecy very popular in Galilee in the first century and explicitly quoted in the New Testament as well as frequently alluded to—it was where a group of fallen angels plummeted to earth. They were said to have given it the name

Hermon from the mutual cursing they flung at each other as they covenanted together to seek the daughters of men as wives.

Those celestial beings were of one heart and one mind too but it wasn't a good one. Covenants aren't always full of light and love.

These fallen angels fathered the giants of old.

Many scholars believe it was on Mount Carmel, not Mount Hermon, the Transfiguration of Jesus took place. On the same mountain as Elijah called down fire from heaven and enacted a victory over the prophets of Baal, Jesus is said to have appeared wrapped in glory, dazzling and bewildering His disciples as He chatted to Moses and Elijah.

Mount Carmel doesn't make sense to me. I agree with those who identify the site of the Transfiguration as Mount Hermon. Not the least of the reasons I consider it more likely is its proximity to Caesarea Philippi.

Only six days prior to Jesus being manifested in glory, Peter had still been Simon. However at Caesarea Philippi, right at the foot of Mount Hermon, Jesus had renamed him. Possibly, given Jesus' subsequent remarks about the gates of hell, they were right outside the temple to Pan—the Roman god from whose name we derive the word *panic*. It was there the gateway to hell was said to be located, marking the entrance to the underworld.

Pan was not actually the god of the underworld—that was Pluto or Hades, whose other name was Dis.

Jesus asked a few leading questions, starting with: 'Who do men say I am?' and culminating with, 'Who do *you* say that I am?'

As a result, Simon had been the first of the disciples to acknowledge Him as the Messiah. Jesus had then called him 'blessed' and given him the name Cephas.

This Hebrew word does not have quite the same meaning as Peter. As I have noted in *God's Poetry*, Peter has the sense of *a stone that marks the beginning of an enterprise.*[45] And that enterprise is the church—the living stones linked to this first and threshold stone—that Jesus instituted as a result of Peter's statement of faith. The words, 'On this rock I will build My church' constitute the moment of conception.

Some scholars believe Peter made his initial statement on Yom Kippur, the Day of Atonement. If this is indeed so, then it is no coincidence that some eight or nine months later comes the feast of Pentecost—the birthday of the church.

Nor is it coincidence that Peter's seemingly witless question six days later was about building shelters for Jesus, Moses and Elijah—because this would have coincided with the Day of Tabernacles, when commemorative huts or shelters were constructed.

Certainly calling Simon by the name Cephas on the Day of Atonement has profound implications. This was a threshold moment, as Jesus indicates by establishing a threshold stone on Simon's words and giving him a threshold name. The name Cephas is redolent of atonement, of covenant, of beginnings.

Covenant: being at one.

Atonement: being at one.

Mount Hermon is not a random place for such a proclamation. The whole landscape resounded in agreement, acting as a cloud of witnesses to Jesus' words.

Mount Hermon is one of the few places in Israel which remains snow-covered all year round. Frost, as you may recall, is *kaphowr*, symbolic of atonement both in its name and white purity.

Kaphowr derives from *kaphar* which has the following meanings and senses: *to cover, coat, coat with pitch, make atonement, to reconcile, purge, pacify, propitiate, forgive, be merciful, cleanse, appease, pardon* and *put off.* It is related to *kapporeth*, the mercy-seat of God and the place of atonement in the Holy of Holies.

As the highest place in Israel as well as a marker for the north, it is a double frontier: both the boundary between Israel and the nations as well as the boundary between heaven and earth.

It's a liminal place, just as a threshold is. Neither in nor out, and yet both in and out.

Of course Jesus went there to talk with Moses and Elijah about what He was to accomplish in Jerusalem the following Passover: the salvation of humanity.

The idea of salvation has changed in the last few centuries. We tend to think salvation is to get us to heaven. But it's far more. It brings heaven down to us.

That's what the transfiguration is all about.

Bringing down heaven to earth.

Jesus was hallowing—and, for that matter, harrowing—the very place where heavenly beings were said to have descended and plotted against humanity.

Jesus took Peter, James and John to prove a point to them: the gates of hell no longer have power here. By implication, the judges who sit in those gates will no longer be the authorities who hold sway on the earth.

The family of Dis, the god of the underworld—disappointment, disease, dismay, disinheritance, disharmony and all their kin—have been disempowered.

Only on reflection would the disciples have understood the message of Jesus: *a new covenant is coming. It is not to replace the law but to nullify your old covenant with death.*

My new covenant will involve blood, salt, name and threshold. When we are one, I will be your covenant defender. I will take on the giants of the land. And even their forefathers who landed on this mountain. They shall not stand.

Be Thou my Vision, O Lord of my heart;
Naught be all else to me, save that Thou art
Thou my best Thought, by day or by night,

Waking or sleeping, Thy presence my light.

Be Thou my Wisdom, and Thou my true Word;
I ever with Thee and Thou with me, Lord;
Thou my great Father, I Thy true son;
Thou in me dwelling, **and I with Thee one.**

Be Thou my Armour, my Sword for the fight;
Be Thou my Dignity, Thou my Delight;
Thou my soul's Shelter, Thou my high Tower:
Raise Thou me heavenward, O Power of my power.

Riches I heed not, nor man's empty praise,
Thou mine Inheritance, now and always:
Thou and Thou only, first in my heart,
High King of heaven, my Treasure Thou art.

High King of heaven, my victory won,
May I reach heaven's joys, O bright heaven's Sun!
Heart of my own heart, *whatever befall,*
Still be my Vision, O Ruler of all.

(Attrib.) Dallan Forgaill
(Tr.) Mary Byrne
(versified) Eleanor Hull

Be Thou My Vision is not a song *about* covenant, it is a song *of* covenant. It is said to have been written by Dallan Forgaill, a chief of the Irish bards in the sixth century. He was also a monk and friend of Columba of Iona.

It's a 'lorica': a breastplate song, a battle hymn, a spiritual covering.[46]

In it there are expressions of the weapon and mantle exchange, the adoption into a new family and acquisition of a new inheritance, the everlasting nature of covenant and the oneness at its heart.

There are also several references to a name covenant and the exchange involved in it, although these are more subtle. Dallan means *blind* and that's what the writer was. So the repetition of vision and the mention of light and sun suggest this was the song by which Dallan Forgaill celebrated his very own individual covenant with God.

Perhaps the most famous lorica of all is *The Deer's Cry*—also called *St. Patrick's Breastplate*—but it does not have the elements of covenant so explicitly lined up as this particular version of *Be Thou My Vision* does.

In many ways, it sums up the essential purpose and sevenfold nature of the blood covenant ceremony.

To go over the main points: when two people sought to become blood brothers, they would undertake a stylised ritual. As part of it, the participants would swear to die for each other, take care of each other's family in the event of the other's death, exchange destinies, confer the dignity of their family and honour of their tribe on the other and swap weapons. The ceremony was called 'cutting a covenant'.

It made two people one.

In our age of fast food and instant everything, many Christians have reduced this complex covenant ceremony with its profoundly rich symbolism, solemn vows and deep profession of commitment to a thirty-second prayer. Often spoken under pressure with dubious motivation.

Does this cut it with God?

Pun fully intended.

No question about it—sometimes it does.

But mostly it doesn't.

The reason why mostly it doesn't is fairly simple.

In Australia, where I live, there are many students who have come across from South-East Asia to go to university. Lots of them encounter Christianity for the first time and decide to become Christians. They'll message home to dad and mum, telling them they have accepted Jesus as Lord and Saviour. No problem! Their parents often approve of this and are sometimes even exceptionally pleased. As far as they are concerned, adding another divinity to the family's pantheon and another line of spiritual insurance is a great idea.

However, everything changes when those new Christian students announce they are going to be baptised. More often than not, their mum or dad will be on a plane the next day, ready to bring them home. What's the difference?

It's an easy distinction. Baptism means *a renunciation of other deities.* To Asian people, it means far more than just repentance for sin. It means a turning away from all divine beings other than the Triune God of the Bible.

In liturgical churches, the rite of baptism does indeed include questions about rejecting and renouncing the satan and all his works and all his empty promises.

This comes *really* close to renouncing the dark covenants that, for many people, exist in their families and govern their lives. But, for some people, it's not close enough.

The satan mimics and mocks God by copying His work. If true covenants can exist—that is, true blood covenants, salt covenants, name covenants and threshold covenants—so too can perversions of them. If true covenants last forever, perversions can last—well, until someone decides to repudiate and renounce them.

In *God's Poetry: The Identity and Destiny Encoded in Your Name*, I explored in detail the most common dark covenant that exists, as well as the way it entwines with name covenants to rob individuals of their destiny.[47] I've looked into the Biblical background of this particular dark covenant, cited as many symptoms as I have observed from my experience of it, as well as explained a way to cut free from it.

It's important to renounce dark covenants because of the oneness intrinsic to the very nature of covenants. Jesus said, 'You cannot serve two masters.'

And you certainly can't be one with both the Light and the Darkness. You can't be one with both Purity and Sin. You can't be one with both Life and Death.

If a dark covenant exists in your family line, it can and will block your oneness with Jesus and thus with the triune God.

Shadow is Light's child. It is nothing without the Light, and nothing if it falls into Darkness.

Anne Hamilton, Many–Coloured Realm

Oneness.

Does it mean giving up individuality? Does becoming corporate mean my unique personality is subsumed into a shared communal whole?

Of course it doesn't.

Paul's image of oneness throughout his writings is that of a body. A foot isn't the same as a hand and an eye can't do the job of an ear or a mouth.

Only when all parts of the body are unified and work together can the whole perform optimally.

I remember hearing a man speak once about the importance of even the smallest parts we might be tempted to overlook. In his youth he'd been a natural runner, fast as the wind, regularly breaking national junior records—and of course he'd had his eye on eventual Olympic selection.

But he'd also been a farm boy and, as a consequence, he'd had a minor accident. A tiny bit of the underside of his little toe had been sliced off when he'd got too close to a sharp tool. It was so miniscule a loss it shouldn't have made the slightest difference to his running ability. But from that point on, he was never as fast. His natural talent wasn't totally lost but he was never again able to achieve the peak performance he had had in the past.

So, whenever you're tempted to think that your contribution to an enterprise won't be missed, think again. Your role might be humble and all but invisible: it might just be that of the little toe that gives a mysterious extra burst of speed and shifts the entire work to a higher gear.

And of course, your role might not be so humble or invisible on a spiritual plane.

When I was a younger Christian I misunderstood the nature of oneness. I felt that giving up my individuality was too big a demand.

I was driving out past Toowoomba, near Gowrie Mountain. I felt lonely in spirit and, as I gazed out on a wash of light over stubbled farmland, an agony of soul threatened to overtake me entirely. 'I can't do it!' I suddenly blurted aloud to God. 'I'm a moth, dazzled by Your flame, a shadow consumed by Your brightness. If I get any closer, I'll be destroyed. Why make me uniquely me if life in its fullness is about giving up being me?'

I honestly didn't expect an answer but I heard a whisper in my mind. 'Come up here and sit beside Me,' He said. 'Let's talk about this.'

'Sit beside You?' I was startled. 'Now? You mean, right now? In-the-middle-of-this-highway-kind-of-now?' I'd never read Ephesians at that point in time and I didn't know about being seated in heavenly places. Sitting next to God seemed rather shocking. All I could think about was James and John, getting their mum to ask if they could sit with Jesus, one on His right hand and one on His left, when He entered His kingdom. Maybe they weren't sitting there, but on the other hand, maybe they were. Jesus didn't really give an unequivocal answer.

One thing was sure, they'd been presumptuous (well, perhaps not entirely so, given the true meaning of the name James[48]) and I certainly didn't want to be. 'You're sure this is ok?'

'Yes. Come on up.' There was a pause as I mentally told whoever was next to the Father to move over, I had an invitation. 'Now, Little Shadow,' He said, 'about shadow.'

'Yes?'

'Shadow is Light's child. There is no shadow unless there is light. No individuality for Annie without the Light. But if shadow falls into darkness, it becomes indistinguishable from it. It is in the dark that shadow ceases to exist, not in the light.'

'I'm not liking this.'

'That's because you prefer the cool and comforting darkness where sin thinks it can conceal itself from Me. You want to be an individual but you also want to hide. These desires, I must tell you, are not compatible.'

'I'm liking this even less.'

'Do you want to go on hiding? Or be an individual?'

I sighed. What an invidious choice. 'Be an individual.' I frowned. It took me half a minute to realise what was wrong. 'Hey, wait up, God! That wasn't the question I asked. I didn't ask about being me but about giving up being me.'

There was silence.

I waited but there was nothing. Then it dawned on me. God had answered my real question, the one I didn't even know my heart was asking.

Oneness with God is not about dissolving my personality into some divine ocean. It's about being called into my true identity in the Body and the Kingdom.

Diogenes Laertius also... says Aristotle... 'being asked what was a friend, answered that it was one soul dwelling in two bodies'.... The Hebrews spake of two friends as being 'one man'. There can be no more striking demonstration of union and love than to say of more than five thousand suddenly drawn together that they had one soul!

Commentary on Acts 4:32—
'All the believers were one in heart and mind.'
Albert Barnes, *Notes on the Bible*

5

Reepicheep's Tail

MY FAVOURITE AUTHOR LIVED in the fourteenth century. I consider him the greatest writer of the last millennium, if not all time. He inspired two of the most influential Christian fiction writers of the twentieth century: JRR Tolkien and CS Lewis. Former children's literature laureate Michael Morpurgo frankly admits he was a reluctant reader (even as an adult) until he happened to encounter the work of this great medieval writer. Morpurgo promptly fell headlong in love with this author's most famous story, finding in it a renewed and rekindled passion for reading.

So, who was this master storyteller of the Middle Ages? Many people have guessed at his name but, the fact is, we're not really sure. He didn't sign the manuscript or tell us his name within it. So he remains anonymous.

What we are sure of is this: he wrote a poem in which troth— or *trawthe*, as he spelt it—was the paramount theme. Troth: the I-will-never-forget-you-I-have-carved-you-on-the-palm-of-my-hand kind of love had, by the late Middle Ages, acquired a sense of honour, truthfulness, commitment and fidelity. It was intimately bound up with a person's faith in God.

Sir Gawain and the Green Knight is the poem in question and in it, truth, love, faith and honour were all explored as troth was put to the test.

The story belongs to the tradition of Arthurian legend and the high tales of Camelot. However it followed a very different treatment to the Arthurian romances circulated by French troubadours of previous centuries.

In *Sir Gawain and the Green Knight*, King Arthur is at table on New Year's Day with his court, waiting for an unusual event to take place. The king has a rule well-known in legend: until a miracle or a marvel occurs, the feasting cannot begin.

Fortunately for the hungry masses, a knight rides into the hall. Both the rider and his horse are green, the colour of magic and the fairy folk. This strange half-giant knight holds an axe in one hand and a holly-branch of peace in the other. He claims the right to a Yuletide game—which he explains like this: if someone will cut off his head, he reserves the right to return the blow in a twelvemonth.

The knights of the Round Table are stunned into silence. After a few well-directed insults from the eldritch knight, Arthur is about to take up the challenge when Gawain steps in to rescue him from obvious folly. He proceeds to behead the giant. The knight's head rolls away but the body quickly picks it up. As the green giant rides off, he reminds Gawain to keep the appointment for the return blow at the Green Chapel, exactly a year hence.

Now Gawain's in a pickle. He's got a year to live. When his head is lopped off, it's going to stay off. He could ignore all that has occurred on the grounds the game was a trick and magic was involved. But he's given his word and considers himself honour-bound.

The seasons roll swiftly past and, as winter approaches, he realises he can delay his departure no longer. So he sets off to find the Green Chapel.

Before he does, there is a long digression. The Arming Sequence describing his gorgeous apparel and detailing, at considerable length, the significance of his heraldic device—the *trawthe*-laden pentangle—is rightly one of the most famous sections of the poem.[49]

When Gawain finally gets on his way, he travels the length of Logres—old Britain—asking everywhere for the whereabouts of the Green Chapel. No one he meets has a clue. He encounters dragons, giants, wood-woses, wild men and the most woeful of weather but there's no sign of the Green Knight. In desperate straits, in the dead of winter, he arrives at the castle of Hautdesert. He is warmly welcomed by the host and his lady as well as a company of visitors who have travelled there for Christmas.

He is feted and feasted for several days and, just as he's explaining why he has to leave, he is informed the Green Chapel is only a short distance away. The host convinces him he should stay, suggesting he rest up the last few days before his fatal appointment at New Year. To lighten the mood and enhance a jovial atmosphere, he then persuades Gawain to take part in a game. The rules are simple: the host is an avid hunter and proposes that whatever he wins the next day during his hunting expedition will be exchanged for whatever Gawain can win during his day of rest.

It all sounds gracious, chivalric and cheerful.

Harmless fun.

A frivolous bargain.

Certainly it doesn't give any appearance of what it actually is: a trap of the most subtle and devious kind. How could it possibly be an attack targeting the heart of Gawain's identity as the man of *trawthe*?

The set-up complete, the host's wife attempts to seduce Gawain. She gets no more than a set of courteous kisses for all her efforts. In accord with the exchange-of-winnings covenant, Gawain passes them on to the host who gives him the spoils of the hunt in return.

The host, laughing, suggests the game go on. And day by day, it does. In addition, the covenants ratifying the agreement to exchange the winnings continue. The fact they are called 'covenants' and sealed with a traditional drink should have alerted Gawain to the fact more was going on than simply a trifling game to while the time away.

However—like many of us in our day–to–day choices—he was oblivious to his own entrapment. The fact that each covenant involved an exchange which included beasts cut in two should have rung warning bells for Gawain. But he is too preoccupied with thoughts of the Green Chapel and the dire fate awaiting him.

He resists temptation—almost to the last.

With the utmost courtesy, he turns down the amorous lady's body as she throws herself at him. He also turns down her glove and ring, the tokens of her love.

However, when she offers a magic girdle to protect him from any weapon, the lure proves too much. Just in case it's a 'jewel for the jeopardy' and can save his head, he decides to keep it. Instead of handing it over according to the rules of the bargain, he conceals it, hoping it will be his salvation during the coming ordeal at the Green Chapel.

New Year's Day finally arrives and he rides off with the green girdle around his waist, dreading the ultimate test of his honour. Too late he realises this test is not ahead, but already behind him.

What appears to have been a literary diversion in the lead-up to the climax turns out to be nothing of the kind. The witty dalliance between Gawain and the host's wife, which seems in line with rambling continental romances, is not a simple courtly interlude at all. Neither is it a natural fall in the tension before a sharp rise to the main crisis of the narrative. It *is* the climax.

The test of troth is not at the sinister Green Chapel but in the bedroom with the lady. *Sir Gawain and the Green Knight* is a tale in which nothing is quite as it seems.

Gawain's heraldic symbol is the pentangle—the five-pointed star of troth. Faithfulness to God, loyalty to his comrades, truthfulness in every circumstance, honour at all times: his armour proclaims him the perfect warrior of God.

Nevertheless he fails.

When it came to the choice between faith and magic, he put his trust, shaky as it was, in the latter.

And so he finally returns to Camelot, a chastened man, wearing the green girdle as a sash: a symbol of penitence and a reminder of his fall. It's a very visible sign of his failure to live up to the highest ideals of the virtue he espoused: when it came to the crunch and he was offered a temptation—a 'magic' girdle to protect him from the axe-wielding Green Knight—he took it and kept it secret, rather than honour his covenant vow and hand it over.

Ultimately he learned that, when cornered—his head about to be on the chopping block—he didn't really trust God nearly as much as he thought he did. The incomparably virtuous Gawain, the peerless knight of matchless integrity, turns out to be 'everyman' in his doubts about God's answers to prayer. Arthur's court, on hearing his story with its confession of unfaith, all join him by wearing green sashes of their own.

They do it with humour, rather than gravity. The Round Table—round so that no knight may be seen to be superior to another—actually approaches an ideal of equality as the knights remind each other they are all sinful: there is a sense of oneness in their solidarity.

Still the story comes from an age when the word 'covenant' was acquiring the sense it generally has today. It was coming closer in meaning to a contract, agreement or bargain. It had not lost its sense of sharing oneness of soul with another, but the shifts were starting.

Nevertheless the medieval era was an age when oneness was of paramount importance; when the cosmos was seen as so interconnected that the consequence of plucking a flower might well be to trouble a star.

The contemporary mindset saw arithmetic, geometry, music, astronomy and theology as a single, seamless integration. Even a frivolous poem like *Sir Gawain and the Green Knight* was built to testify to such oneness as well as expound Paul's exposition of the Armour of God.

I suspect it is the closing incident of Round Table solidarity in *Sir Gawain and the Green Knight* that inspired CS Lewis to include a scene I particularly cherish in *Prince Caspian*.

Jack Lewis[50] wrote both my favourite and least favourite children's books. In *Prince Caspian*, he introduces Reepicheep, one of the most heroic characters in the entire seven-volume *Narnia Chronicles*.

Like Gawain in *Sir Gawain and the Green Knight*, Reepicheep is a truly 'gentil parfait knight', the very epitome of dauntless courage and virtuous integrity. Unlike Gawain, Reepicheep doesn't fall. His virtue remains intact, his honour is never dimmed. He's such a perfect gentleman, it's a pity he's a mouse.

Or maybe not.

The perfect mouse whose faith never fails is one thing, the perfect person quite another. As Gawain would readily testify.

Reepicheep has many fine moments. My favourite is the scene where he loses his tail in battle and then asks a boon of Aslan: to restore the stump on his rump to its former glory.

When Aslan points out that Reepicheep puts too much store by his tail, the company of Talking Mice all draw their swords. It seems they are about to attack—but no. It's to cut off their own tails.

If the Chief Mouse is to be without the honour of a tail, one of them explains, then they will join him in disgrace.

The company of mice, like Arthur's knights of the Round Table and the band of Musketeers invented by Alexandre Dumas, are solidly 'all for one and one for all'. That's really just another way of expressing 'heart of my own heart'.

Aslan, disarmed by the great hearts of the mice and their love for their leader, yields to the claim. He restores Reepicheep's tail.

Whenever I think of this part of *Narnian Chronicles*, I'm always reminded of a company of four men. And no—that company isn't D'Artagnan and the Three Musketeers.

These four were real people. Like the author of *Sir Gawain and the Green Knight*, their names have been lost to history. They are remembered, however, for digging a hole in a roof. They had a friend who was paralysed and they were sure that, if only they could get him to Jesus, all would be well.

However the crowds around Jesus made it impossible to approach Him. They simply couldn't get through the front door to the place He was staying. So, in a moment of desperation and inspiration, they took him up to the flat-topped roof typical of Jewish houses at the time, and started to rip it up.

Once the hole in the roof was big enough, they carefully lowered their paralysed friend down through it on a mat.

Jesus, in healing the man, seemed to be responding to the faith of the friends. Just as He responded to the faith of the centurion who asked on behalf of his servant.

So often it's not about the faith of the individual who needs healing. Sometimes we need to hold others in our hearts and have faith for them when they are, for whatever reason, incapable of doing so themselves.

It's not unscriptural to have faith on behalf of another.

And yet...

...we have to be extremely careful.

The faith of friends is a temporary measure, no long-term substitute for developing our own deeper relationship with God.

Burden-bearing can go too far. CS Lewis, brilliant as he was at apologetics and at setting out Christianity in plain vanilla wrapping for skeptics to grasp, made this mistake. Influenced by the theology of Charles Williams, he was glad at the prospect of bearing his wife's pain while she was dying of cancer.

However, we are not called to substitutionary atonement. That is the work of Jesus Himself. We usurp His role if we try to take on any burden—physical, emotional, mental, spiritual—for another person He has not given us.

Bear one another's burdens.

Each man should bear his own burden.

There's no contradiction here.

Some people want to off-load the whole of their appointed burden onto others. They don't want to bear their own burden, let alone share those of others.

Other people have made it their life's role to take on the pain of others, to shoulder all of their own burden and also that of those around them. They do it so continually it can eventually become so much part of who they are that they can't stop helping, even when they know they should. Even when it's too much and they're close to breakdown.

The first sort of people are leeches who suck others dry. The others are like pelicans who, so medieval people believed, would—when all else failed—stab themselves to offer their lifeblood to feed the birds around them.

Make no mistake about it: there are people, like King Saul, who use the notion of covenant for their own ends. If they're involved in one, it's for what they can get out of it, not for what they can put in. They want to be lifted up but the prospect of lifting up others in turn is not part of their plan. They ignore the aspect of mutuality all armour-bearing implies.

We're not called to be like leeches or pelicans, but geese.

It's not about individuality, but formation.

There are some men who lift the age they inhabit, till all men walk on higher ground in that lifetime.

Maxwell Anderson

God's Panoply

In Celtic spirituality, the wild goose is the symbol of the Holy Spirit. The harsh cold of the north is not a climate suited to doves, and the Gaels, in choosing a new emblem, could hardly have done better: the oneness of relationship within the Trinity is reflected by the oneness of flying geese. It's a pale reflection admittedly but, as we've seen before, even geese tell us about the nature of God.

'Look at the birds in the sky!' Jesus said.

So let's go back to the geese of the north and examine their lifestyle again.

Every formation has a goose out front on point. He's the head of the wedge, the tip of the arrowhead. As the first, he's 'covering' for the others. As the one who leads and sets the pace, he doesn't enjoy the uplift that those behind do. There's no one ahead of him to be the wind beneath his wings. He does it tough.

He cuts the headwinds and shields the formation as he drives through storm and snow. It's exhausting to be the one out front, having to put in the extra effort, having to persevere, endure and keep flying unswervingly in the right direction.

From time to time, he'll slip back into the rear of the formation while another goose takes the front position. Geese have got the whole concept of nasa' down to a fine art: they stand in for each other to preserve the formation and reach their destination.

Incidentally they demonstrate the truth of Paul's statement: 'The whole body [is] held together by what every joint supplies, according to the proper working of each individual part...'

Ephesians 4:16 NAS

This wonderful covenant image of individual members making up one body is reflected by the geese in their flying wedge. In that wedge, there are older geese, sick geese and young fledglings. None of these will get a turn up front. They'll be continually protected at the back, given the uplift they need to help them during the flight. They are not, however, bumming a lift.

They're the cheer squad.

Inevitably, at some stage, the going will get tough. And the goose at point will be doing it tough. The lead might exchange several times as bad weather makes the flight more and more perilous. A storm front might loom, icy winds might sweep over the wedge, pushing them off-course.

It's then the cheer squad comes into its own. First there's a lone honk from the rear of the formation. Then a chorus of encouragement as the geese up the back honk in unison to the leaders. Occasionally there's a strident grumbler in the wedge, but his complaints will get drowned out by the honks of support.

This is another aspect of nasa': to '...encourage one another and build each other up...' as Paul wrote to the Thessalonians.[51] Paul himself had experienced just this sort of uplift and support.

Well over a decade after he was blinded on the road to Damascus, he was a nobody. He'd slipped into obscurity. If anyone remembered him at all, it was for his role in the persecution of the church after the death of Stephen.

Then Joseph went looking for him. Joseph was nicknamed Barnabas, *son of encouragement*. Seeing his potential, Barnabas sponsored him and took him to see the apostles.

Paul of Tarsus eventually changed the world. But only because of the uplift and prayerful backing Barnabas gave him.

My mum often tells the story of how she and dad had decided, after months of heartache and problems in the Christian ministry they were involved with, to just pull the plug and say their goodbyes. They had discussed it over a long period of time and finally, towards midnight one night, made their decision to hand in their resignations the next day.

No sooner had they done so than the phone rang. 'What are you doing?' asked an agitated voice at the other end. 'Sorry to ring so late but we felt it couldn't wait.'

My mum recognised the voice of a woman she'd ministered to

for cult involvement some years previously.

The woman went on. 'Our small group has been praying for you two for the last three weeks and tonight we felt some urgency, so we gave over the entire prayer session to you both. We believe we have a special message for you from God. *But what are you doing?*'

Mum explained that she and dad had only just that moment made the decision to leave the ministry.

'Well,' said the woman. 'The message makes sense then. It's this: *most people do not receive the blessing God wants them to have, because they give up too soon.*'

Paul tells us in Galatians that we reap a harvest of blessing if we do not give up.[52]

Harvest is an interesting word. It implies sowing seed, watering it, weeding, tending... In our instant age, we tend to believe that we can go from seed to harvest in an hour or two.

We need instead to remember Paul's words to the Thessalonians: '*Do not grow weary in doing good.*'[53] We need those who act like honking geese and say, 'Be encouraged. We're right behind you! We've got you covered!'

We both need them for ourselves and need to be like them for others.

We live in an age when Christians think they can fly solo. Hurt by other members of the church but still loving Jesus, many people just opt out. But faith is meant to upbuild each other, exhort each other, correct and warn and encourage each other. Faith is not meant to be exercised in isolation.

'The eye cannot say to the hand, "I don't need you!" And the head cannot say to the feet, "I don't need you!"' (1 Corinthians 12:21 NIV)

We're meant to be part of a Body. We're meant to provide uplift for one another. We're called over and over again to oneness, not aloneness.

Two friends, one soul.

Euripides

quoted by John O'Donohue, *Anam Cara*

Some people have a head-start on armour-bearing and oneness. They are naturals when it comes to bearing the burdens of others. True and right burden-bearing is when Jesus moves through us to draw to Himself those whose life-wounds need to be healed.

It is a gift.

Some people are born with it. Unredeemed, however, it can break the very people it is meant to serve. If you have the gift, you sense the emotions and feelings of those around you without necessarily being aware that is what you are doing. You might be labelled 'sensitive', perhaps even the 'designated patient' of the family.

Burden-bearing is a gift for those especially called to intercessory prayer on behalf of others. But, instead of that happening, it may result in wounding and isolation. In extreme cases, people can be so receptive to the pain of others, they cut themselves off from normal society to keep their sanity.

Or, alternatively, the natural compassion of burden-bearers can draw them into the error of substitutionary at–one–ment, where they take on the suffering of someone they love or pity. As previously mentioned, even CS Lewis fell into this trap.

We are called to represent Christ, not usurp His role as kinsman-redeemer.

I know of no finer explanation about burden-bearing, how it should be done rightly and the damage we can inflict on ourselves if we adopt it wrongly, than that by John and Paula Sandford in *Letting Go of Your Past.*[54]

Jesus said that His yoke is easy and His burden is light—but if it isn't for you—then it may be that your gift of burden-bearing is presently unredeemed.

For people with this gift, its fleshly aspects need to be dealt with and cut away and it requires surgery by the Holy Spirit before going into covenantal oneness.

Literature is a luxury; fiction is a necessity.

GK Chesterton

When we lose an understanding of what covenant means and what oneness is all about, it affects our culture down to the deepest levels. Even down to the way we read and write stories.

It amazes me that some people never read fiction. They miss out on the joy of stories like *Sir Gawain and the Green Knight*, the *Chronicles of Narnia*, *The Three Musketeers*. More importantly, they miss out on the experience of oneness and the multiple levels of corporateness offered by good literature.

Penelope Lively commented in *Enchanted Hunters* that she believes the almost-miraculous ability of children to fuse with the narrative and get inside the skin of a character is irretrievably lost as we grow older. Detached, objective and critical reading destroys that knack forever.

Poor Penelope! Just because she lost the ability to fuse with the story doesn't mean all adults have. A contrary view is offered by Orson

Scott Card in *Meditations on Middle Earth* in which he points out it is in reading fiction we come closest, however briefly, to being of 'one mind'.

He notes that the side-effects of this approach to a single worldview are well-documented by researchers: overwhelmingly, fiction readers are apt to be more understanding of others and their viewpoints, more empathetic in their dealings with others' feelings and less liable to believe their own position is totally and immaculately right.

According to Card, the great gift of fiction is the possibility of achieving authentic communication as well as true concord of worldview through the sharing of memories shaped by the author.

And beyond the author's interaction with an individual reader lies the possibility of a united body of readers, abuzz with the common shared story.

Of course not all fiction creates these opportunities. Still the best of it does.[55]

Over many years of reviewing books I came to realise not everyone enters into story. However I thought they were unaware of their loss, except in rare cases like Penelope Lively.

Until I read Card's article, it had never occurred to me there are people in the world who deliberately detach themselves from a story. It was a stunning moment of revelation when I discovered the existence of readers who not only didn't regret such a disconnection but actively desired it. Moreover they were contemptuous of those who fell into the trap of 'naïve identification' and read from the inside of a story rather than its outside.

Card calls them 'literadors': people who treat story-reading like a bullfight. Examining the text in a post-modern milieu, perpetually removed from it, they're out for the clean kill as they flash their critical skill.

Now whenever I analyse literature and dig into its mathematical underpinnings, my purpose is to head deeper into the oneness, not farther away from it. I want to retain that sense of being like a little child, along with the wonder of it all.

As Card points out, 'serious' readings of literature result in scholarly papers while 'escapist' readings result in experiences so powerful they cannot be codified. The aloof, detached observer-reader looking in on the story from the exterior will never be changed by it.

But those of us who read it from the inside like a little child always run the danger of never being quite the same person at story's end.

Fiction is valued in every human society precisely because it makes us who read it temporarily, approximately, One.

Orson Scott Card, *Meditations on Middle Earth*

It wasn't so very many generations ago society as a whole still valued truth and saw it as an absolute. Then the trickle of postmodernism became a rising tide, truth became relative and people began to value what was 'real' instead.

'Get real' was the motto of the times as it became clear the individual's perception of what was real trumped any claims of absolute truth. *Coca-cola* popularised the trend with its slogan: *It's the real thing.* Variations on that theme lasted two decades.

Today, 'real' is as obsolete as 'true'.

Western youth are generally oblivious to either. So many of them have been raised by parents who have denied them nothing that they expect to get what they want when they want it without having to work for it. In the past, such expectations were confined to the aristocracy. Indeed, this generation behaves as entitled, if not titled.

They feel entitled to a first home like the one their parents finished with, to a high-salaried career with days off at whim. Recently a friend commented that one of his friends had quit his job to go on welfare so he could play more X-Box.

How on earth can we explain *grace* to this kind of mentality?

There is no entitlement with grace. They are antithetical.

How can we talk identity or destiny with an entire generation intent on the self-centred pursuit of entertainment?

Past generations were concerned with the true or the real. This one is only concerned with fun. They are often violently resistant to the 'serious' message of grace, peace and hope in the Gospel.

Yet there is an avenue to approach them: through the medium of *story*.

For many years, some pioneering New Zealanders have evangelised the sort of kids whose lives revolve around drag-racing on Saturday nights.

By anchoring their own story in that of Genesis–to–Revelation, they've had astonishing success.

I don't find this all that remarkable.

Because it is in story we approach the ideal of oneness.

At one magical instant in your early childhood, the page of a book— that string of confused, alien ciphers—shivered into meaning. Words spoke to you, gave up their secrets... whole universes opened.

Alberto Manguel

I could hear my class coming from two blocks away. They were marching along, arms linked, chanting at the top of their voices. As they approached, I realised it was going to be one of *those* days. It was my all-girls class and every single one of them was a problem child. On a good day, it was like wrangling zoo animals, on a bad day... a bit like trying to tackle the psychotic killer penguins in the movie *Madagascar*.

It was only as the girls arrived at the classroom door I realised their chant was actually a poem. I hesitate to immortalise the last two lines of this inglorious ditty but it's the only way to explain their manic glee as they halted on the top step:

'So I made a pass
At his gorgeous arse.'

I'm not sure, I thought to myself, what the rules of this game are. So I'd better play along until I do.

I raised my eyebrows, put on a shocked look and adopted a disapproving tone. 'What on earth is the meaning of this?'

They had a spokesperson lined up. 'We're practising for our test, Miss.'

'You expect me to believe that?'

'It's an English test, Miss. Performance poetry. Group recitation.'

'Did I come down in the last rainshower?'

'You can check with our English teacher, Miss.'

'I will. Who is your English teacher and what is the name of this alleged poem?'

The moment they said their teacher's name, I knew I didn't have to check. They were undoubtedly telling the truth. They've got me, I thought. Hoist on my own petard. And they know it. That's why they're so infernally smug.

One of my classroom rules was this: if you happen to have a

test in the period following, you can ask for a reduced workload. As soon as you get your exercises done, you can take out the work you need to study for your test and do it instead of mathematics.

It didn't happen often and it usually involved only a few students at a time. But this was the whole class.

We did a deal.

They'd complete an exercise on ratio and proportion, then they'd all stand to practise the group recitation; another exercise, another practice. At the end of a double period, they'd ploughed through more mathematics than they had in several weeks. But they'd also, with malicious grins and abominable delight, had a dozen opportunities to practise their performance piece.

I was not surprised to learn several days later they were the highest scoring group in their year level on this particular test.

I took my shattered nerves to the staffroom when it was all over and wailed: 'Ten centuries of glorious English poetry and I have to put up with *So I made a pass at his gorgeous arse* ad nauseum.'

My colleagues were completely unsympathetic. 'Get used to it,' said Shaun. 'You know what's happened in that new pilot project? We just heard: all but four kids in Year Nine failed mathematics.'

I was stunned. Nearly three hundred students in a single year level at a nearby new state-of-the-art college hadn't passed ordinary arithmetic. It was an inconceivable percentage. 'How is that possible?'

'Their integrated theme was *puppets*, that's how.'

By this stage, Shaun had the attention of the entire staffroom. We'd all been teaching long enough to know about pilot projects. They were like Pharoah's battles: invariably a resounding success, whatever the outcome. 'How long have we got before we get a departmental directive to implement it?'

'Six months, if we're lucky.'

Over lunch we discussed how to avoid a similar fiasco.

We were all in agreement that the golden ratio was the best teaching tool from a mathematical point of view: you could approach it from the angle of a quadratic equation just as easily as you could introduce it from simple addition. Moreover we could look at its use in art, in the natural world, in ancient architecture—it would give us a point of access to many other subjects and enable us to start building an integrated curriculum.

There was one flaw in all this and we knew it. Without the English Department on board, we wouldn't be able to implement the plan. And, in those days before *The Da Vinci Code*, none of us knew of any literature which featured the golden ratio.

That night I received an email from a friend of mine who knew nothing of all this. He thought I'd be interested in an article which had appeared in *The Times* about an Australian researcher who had discovered a golden ratio structure in some medieval French literature.

The trap—and in retrospect I have to suspect it was a divine one—was set. Having been subjected to a double period of suggestive chanting followed by the news of an impending teaching disaster, I had serious incentive to look at medieval poetry in a way I doubt anyone has ever done before.

I was looking for poems that young teens might enjoy but I also specifically wanted to find literature with a mathematical structure the average thirteen year old could analyse. I soon stumbled across a niche world of very specialised scholarship.

There are experts in the mathematical structure of literature. They notice really odd things.

Like:

- there are three collections of six verse types totalling 6666 letters
- this poem has an old word for Pythagoras' famous theorem about the sides of a triangle in just the right position for such a triangle embedded in the text structure
- John's Gospel starts with a 496-syllable poem and finishes with a 496-word epilogue, also positioning the 'disciple

Jesus loved' at the end to mirror-reflect the name John at the beginning and thereby confirming the identity of the writer

And that was just for starters! Oh, wow! Opened to me was a world in which people had not only believed in the oneness of words and numbers but had acted on their belief. It was like the clouds parting so I could catch a glimpse in the distance of a mathematical Everest I hadn't even known existed. Around it were the glittering peaks of an entire numerical mountain range. I was touching heaven.

One thing was missing.

As I flung myself headlong into reading this research, I noticed that almost no one was asking the obvious questions.

Why?

What is the significance of these particular numbers?

Now, because I was looking for dead-simple patterns even the least mathematically-minded of my students could spot, I discovered structures everyone else seemed to have overlooked.

Why were so many medieval poems multiples of 22? Was it because there are 22 letters in the Hebrew alphabet?

Why did 'troth' turn up so often at the golden ratio? Is it significant that the golden ratio was so important to the Greeks it was effectively termed 'the logos'?

490 turned up a lot as the size of poems or sub-sections—surely that would be seventy times seven and symbolic of forgiveness.

So, were these poets simply making biblical allusions via their number choices?

It was an entirely different way of thinking. It was a world in which mathematics was no longer set apart, lofty and serene, but one in which both arithmetic and geometry were allied to music and astronomy, and in which numbers acted as theological metaphors.

We live in a world where fragmentation reigns supreme. Various branches of science advance at a swift pace to a large extent because of specialisation. This leads to a way of thinking entirely at odds with that of the past. Even though our age knows of the 'butterfly effect', we have largely abandoned that medieval notion that the final result of plucking a flower may be unsettling a star. We no longer think our actions might have cosmic consequences.

This was not the case in the past where every action was seen as having a reaction. And that reaction another reaction.

Everything was related, inter-connected: even the numerical literary art practised in the poems of the Middle Ages was meant to express the covenantal oneness of a redeemed creation.

It probably won't surprise you right at this moment to know the length of each section in this book is chosen with deliberate thought as to its mathematical structure. The third section of the first chapter is about forgiveness and is 490 words long. The two preceding sections are both 333 words.

The sections about armour are generally 777 words; those about covenant are variously 333, 444, 555, 777, 888, 999 or 1111 words long. The desired word length for some of the chapters is made up by those quotes that divide sections. I've even used the golden ratio from time to time, so that one section and a succeeding section are in that 'divine proportion'.

Eventually why I chose these numbers will become clear. I got them from the author of *Sir Gawain and the Green Knight* and he got them from the New Testament, mainly from Paul's letters.

Modern translations of the Bible do not take any of its mathematical structure into account. It doesn't seem to even enter a translator's head to make the attempt to keep any of the numerical formatting.

The opening of the letter to the Ephesians might be noteworthy for its 202-word Greek sentence[56] extending from verse 3 to verse

14, but only because it's such a mammoth mouthful! Not because anyone thinks there is any special significance in the number 202.

(Actually, I believe 202 is tremendously significant. Multiples of 101 occur throughout *Sir Gawain and the Green Knight* and the other poems in the same manuscript. In that context, 101 is a vastly mysterious number to most commentators. Why it isn't 100 baffles them. Leaving aside its meaning, I was immediately suspicious my favourite poet knew why Paul of Tarsus used 202 and might have copied the sense. This also suggested to me I'd find another multiple of 101 reflected at the end of Ephesians in the *Armour of God* sequence. A quick search turned up the fact that Ephesians 6:13–18 is 101 words in Greek. This takes the allusions in the passage to a whole new level.)

Our complete disregard for the mathematics of a text was not an attitude shared by all translators of the past.

When Jerome translated the Greek and Hebrew text into Latin in the fourth century, he tried to preserve both the overall sense of the words as well as that of the numbers.[57] The Vulgate text he produced was to receive immense criticism in the age of the Protestant Reformers. However, it's worth recognising he faced an insurmountable translation challenge. In his time—as it was for over a millennium previously and would be for over another millennium—words and numbers were inseparable companions.

The question of which was more important would not have made sense to the people of that age: there were no distinct numerical digits in either Greek or Hebrew. The letters of the alphabet served a dual purpose: they had both a literary and a mathematical function.

Numbers and words were a fusion. The present separation of mathematics and language was unthinkable.

Today we tend to think of a scribe as someone who writes words. The word has no mathematical connotation at all. However the Hebrew scribes, famously depicted in the gospels as attempting to entrap Jesus, were the Sopherim, *the counters*. Their name comes from 'caphar', *to count, number, enumerate exactly* but also means *to recount* or *talk.*

In ensuring the accuracy of Scriptural copying, they used mathematics as a back-up. They didn't just simply count: complex numerical designs were part and parcel of their cross-checking.

Today, even those who acknowledge the Greek term, *logos*, has a sense of both word and number tend to ignore the mathematical aspect. Because *logos* is universally translated 'Word' in the opening to John's Gospel, it is stripped of all other associations. When the Greeks, however, were referring to a numerical concept as THE *logos*, they meant the geometrical formulation now called the 'golden ratio'.

As David Howlett has shown in *British Books in Biblical Style*, the golden ratio (or *the logos*) is integral to the design of the Hebrew text for the sequence of 'days' in the first chapter of Genesis. Furthermore he has also shown that Jerome tried to keep a similar design in the Vulgate by imitating that word–number fusion.

The golden ratio is a vastly more significant find in Genesis than the number seven is. Seven, dare I say it, has nothing to do with 'completeness'.[58] Rather it is 'rest' as well as a stunning combination of the two fundamental design principles of the universe: the golden ratio with Isaac Newton's famous inverse square law. Every created thing shows evidence of a tendency towards the golden ratio somewhere in its design: it doesn't matter whether it's daisies or comets, shells or bananas, parrots or sheep, hurricanes or butterflies, snowflakes or beehives, feathers or claws, galaxies or chromosomes.

I believe absolutely everything is marked somewhere with the numerical *logos*. Absolutely *every*thing. In *The Singing Silence* I point out this universality of our Creator's mark. There I also suggest an analysis of the mathematics itself testifies to three aspects of His nature: He is a Trinity, He is Love and He is Resurrection and Life.

In choosing the word 'logos' to open his gospel, John points directly to the mathematical design of Genesis and to the hallmark of the Creator. It's well-known he echoed the *verbal* content of Genesis but there remain unplumbed *arithmetical* deeps in John's opening 'Hymn to the Logos'.

I hope you begin to understand why I've used this ancient technique of 'numerical literary design' or 'Biblical style' throughout this book. If I'm going to talk about covenantal oneness, how can I possibly conform to the canons of this present age which decree a separation of words and numbers? I'm as serious about what I do as Paul was when he chose his multiples of 101 at the beginning and end of Ephesians.

Every section so far in this book is designed to reflect, in its underlying mathematics, something significant about God's nature.

If you really want to rile me, you'll call it numerology. It's not. It's numerical art. I'm certainly nowhere near as good at it as Paul or John or even Matthew, but I make the effort to marry my words and numbers, rather than to go along with their present-day widely-accepted divorce.

Nevertheless, if this work were to be translated into another language, I wouldn't expect the translators to keep the numerical formatting.

It's simply not that important an element in this day and age.

But what is currently the case was not always true.

Forgiveness is the power,
And forgiveness the arena
For the lives of perfect men
Who are bound to Me by love
In My strong, new covenant,
In this furious dance called life,

God's Panoply

Where I never let you go
As My hand clenches yours.

Norman Habel,
Are You Joking, Jeremiah?

It possibly hasn't been obvious but, for several chapters, I've been laying down blocks of a huge jigsaw. You may have thought large chunks of this book are unconnected. You may even have thought that, for someone who likes to go on about oneness, I should have kept to one track. But linear thinking didn't seem the right way to recreate a concept as paradoxical as the one I'm about to unveil.

Ready?

Take a good look at this last piece of the jigsaw.

In the Middle Ages, mathematics was considered the language of heaven. Arithmetic, geometry, music and astronomy were studied as a unified whole. (With music and astronomy in that mix, it's obvious how 'the language of heaven' idea arose.) Within the numerical design of some medieval poems, there are references to a beautiful concept the authors connected to *nasa'* and *submission*.

Because, as far as I am aware, you won't find this concept in theology anywhere today but only in the mathematical-literary fusions of yesterday, I've taken the trouble to explain the background at length.

A thousand years ago, a Jewish teaching of the first century emerged from its chrysalis and took full flight into Christendom. It had such an impact that, for nearly half a millennium, it dominated Christian artistic expression in the west.

The teaching's appeal lay in its embrace of the paradoxical nature of God—both fully merciful and fully just.

In Greek logic, mercy and justice are incompatible. But not in Hebrew thinking!

The original first-century Jewish teaching focussed on creation—however, the theme of the medieval Christian version was usually redemption.

Here is (more-or-less[59]) that original:

> God was just about to create Adam but not all the angels were wholly in favour of the prospect. Some agreed, 'Create him,' while others were against it. It is obvious there was contention amongst the heavenly hosts because in Psalm 85:10 it is written, 'Mercy and truth fought, justice and peace went into combat.'

> Mercy thus clearly said, 'Create him, because he will practise mercy.' Truth was against this: 'Don't create him! He will practise lies.' Justice took sides with Mercy: 'Do it, because he will be just.' Peace opposed them: 'Don't, because he will bring war and strife.'

> What did God do in response to this angelic argument? He threw Truth down to earth, as Daniel 8:12 says. The angels were baffled. 'Master of the universe,' they dared ask, 'why did you despise your seal and your first bodyguard, Truth? Let Truth arise from the earth.' So it is written in Psalm 85:11, 'Let truth spring up from the earth.'

There isn't a single English translation today where Psalm 85:10–11 says, 'Mercy and truth fought, justice and peace went into combat. Let truth arise from the earth.'

The majority are along these lines: *Mercy and Truth meet together, Peace and Justice kiss each other. Faithfulness springs forth from the earth and righteousness looks down from heaven.*

This beautiful verse is about reconciliation while the former is about the inherent opposition between mercy and justice.

Can both be right? Can both *kiss* and *combat* be correct? Although it seems impossible to resolve the paradox, yes. Here is an extreme case, a translation problem similar to that we saw with איל (ayil): *oak, ram, deer, morning star.*

The seemingly-contrary concepts within this verse exercised the best creative minds of the medieval era. The result of their endeavours was the '*Four Daughters of God*', a theme running like a golden thread through poetry, drama, theology and even—incredibly—land measurement.

Yet can kissing and fighting truly be reconciled into a single concept? Is it possible?

Let's turn our minds once more to armour–bearing.

> *Here is love, vast as the ocean,*
> *Loving–kindness as the flood,*
> *When the Prince of Life, our Ransom,*
> *Shed for us His precious blood.*
> *Who His love will not remember?*
> *Who can cease to sing His praise?*
> *He can never be forgotten,*
> *Throughout heav'n's eternal days.*
>
> *On the mount of crucifixion,*
> *Fountains opened deep and wide;*
> *Through the floodgates of God's mercy*
> *Flowed a vast and gracious tide.*
> *Grace and love, like mighty rivers,*

Poured incessant from above,
And heav'n's peace and perfect justice
Kissed a guilty world in love.

Gwilym Hiraethog[60]

The story of the arguing angels begins with Rabbi Simon in the first century. I'd like to think he was well-acquainted with Saul of Tarsus. If they weren't familiar with each other, then Simon's midrash must have been incredibly famous to have influenced Saul's thinking over such a long time. Traces of it can be found in Ephesians, Romans, 2 Corinthians and 1 Thessalonians.[61]

Today, this same story is related in Jewish catechisms.[62]

In the Middle Ages, however, this story began to make an impact through two famous sermons delivered around the same time: one by Hugh of St Victor and the other by Bernard of Clairvaux.

The question of how God's justice can be reconciled with mercy exercised the minds and imagination of generations of creative artists. If God is fully just and punishes sin with complete impartiality and total righteousness, there is no real place for mercy in the universe. Yet if God is thoroughly merciful, then justice is undermined. If indeed God is willing to offer mercy to every individual, then the concept of justice becomes nonsense.

Yet God is both fully just and fully merciful.

This is a paradox.

At least it is in Greek thinking. And in Greek thinking, as we have noted, a paradox is a problem: it is used to demonstrate the falsity of an argument. (It can be used to prove truth too but by producing a logical paradox to show it can't be false.) Hebrew thinking took paradox in its stride.

By the time of the Middle Ages, a thousand years of Greek-style thinking had influenced the church. God's justice and mercy were seen in the light of paradox. And perhaps it was for this very reason that Rabbi Simon's story was to inspire centuries of artistic expression when applied to mankind's redemption.

There were as many versions of the *Four Daughters of God* as there were story-tellers.[63] However a general outline goes like this:

Lady Mercy threatens to leave heaven in a huff because Father God has been so righteous in his judgments there's no place for her anymore. Lady Truth tries to persuade her differently. When Lady Justice arrives to add her thoughts to the mix, the discussion comes to blows. Lady Peace tries to calm the situation down but her efforts are rebuffed and she decides to leave with Lady Mercy. Enter, stage right, the Son of Man with a plan. Jesus proposes to redeem the world, His wisdom is acclaimed and all are reconciled in a loving kiss.

The inspiration for this was Rabbi Simon's personification of the virtues and the key elements from Psalm 85:10–11. Let's see what our modern translators have devised for these verses. If I've left out your favourite translation, it's probably because it's identical to another:

Mercy and loving–kindness and truth have met together; righteousness and peace have kissed each other. Truth shall spring up from the earth, and righteousness shall look down from heaven.

Amplified Bible (AMP)

Mercy and faith have come together; righteousness and peace have given one another a kiss. Faith comes up from the earth like a plant; righteousness is looking down from heaven.

Bible in Basic English (BBE)

Faithful love and truth have met; righteousness and peace have kissed. Truth springs up from the ground; righteousness gazes down from heaven.

Common English Bible (CEB)

Love and loyalty will come together; goodness and peace will unite. Loyalty will sprout from the ground; justice will look down from the sky above.

Contemporary English Version (CEV)

Grace and truth have met together; justice and peace have kissed each other. Truth springs up from the earth, and justice looks down from heaven.

Complete Jewish Bible (CJB)

Mercy and truth have met. Righteousness and peace have kissed. Truth sprouts from the ground, and righteousness looks down from heaven.

GOD'S WORD Translation (GWT)

Love and faithfulness will meet; righteousness and peace will embrace. Human loyalty will reach up from the earth, and God's righteousness will look down from heaven.

Good News Translation (GNT)

Faithful love and truth will join together; righteousness and peace will embrace. Truth will spring up from the earth, and righteousness will look down from heaven.

Holman Christian Standard Bible (HCSB)

Mercy and truth are met together; righteousness and peace have kissed each other. Truth shall spring out of the earth; and righteousness shall look down from heaven.

King James Version (KJV)

Lovingkindness and truth have met together; Righteousness and peace have kissed each other. Truth springs from the earth, and righteousness looks down from heaven.

New American Standard (NAS)

Love and truth belong to God's people; goodness and peace will be theirs. On earth people will be loyal to God, and God's goodness will shine down from heaven.

New Century Version (NCV)

Unfailing love and truth have met together. Righteousness and peace have kissed! Truth springs up from the earth, and righteousness smiles down from heaven.

New Living Translation (NLT)

Love and faithfulness meet together; righteousness and peace kiss each other. Faithfulness springs forth from the earth, and righteousness looks down from heaven.

New International Version (NIV)

God's truth and faithful love join together. His peace and holiness kiss each other. His truth springs up from the earth. His holiness looks down from heaven.

New International Reader's Version (NIRV)

Steadfast love and faithfulness will meet; righteousness and peace will kiss each other. Faithfulness will spring up from the ground, and righteousness will look down from the sky.

New Revised Standard (NRS)

Mercy and truth met themselves; rightfulness and peace were kissed. (Love and faithfulness came together; righteousness and peace kissed each other.) Truth came forth (out) of the earth; and rightfulness beheld from heaven. (Faithfulness sprang forth from the earth; and righteousness looked down from heaven.)

Wycliffe (WYC)

Almost the only word the translators are all agreed on is *peace*. This is why it's worthwhile checking out different Bible versions. They shed different light on the fine nuances of the language. This is true in the New Testament as well, where the koine Greek—or street lingo—of the day was given a distinct literary edge.

Back in the Middle Ages, we wouldn't have had as much difficulty translating the Hebrew word *chesed* as we do today when we look at all the variants proposed: *truth, faith, faithful love, faithfulness, loyalty, lovingkindness.*

Yes, back then we could have chosen *troth.*

Troth: that very special virtue the author of *Sir Gawain and the Green Knight* teased out with such finesse.

Troth: that very special virtue testified to by the heraldry of Gawain's surcoat and shield with their logos-drenched pentangles.

Troth: that very special virtue that implied Gawain was a covenant-keeping man.

I will betroth you to Me forever; Yes, I will betroth you to Me in righteousness and justice, in lovingkindness and mercy... and you shall know the Lord.

Hosea 2:19–20 NKJV

The anonymous author of *Sir Gawain and the Green Knight* was obviously, at least to me, a great admirer of Paul's writing. In particular, he had an especial fondness for Ephesians 6:13–18—the Armour of God.

In his poetry, he mathematically linked Gawain's armour, and particularly his shield and its emblem, to the Four Daughters of God.

When I first noticed this, I thought I'd made a mistake. Or that the poet had. But I'd developed a lot of respect for this man's intelligence, so I kept looking. And the more I looked, the deeper the connections became.

However it still didn't make any sense to bind together Ephesians 6 and Psalm 85:10–11. At least initially. I racked my brains for several months. Then, finally, I noticed several fascinating parallels. They were so obvious that, in retrospect, I was chagrined at how long it took me to spot them:

The Four Daughters of God	The Armour of God
Lady Mercy (Faithful love)	The Shield of Faith
Lady Truth	The Belt of Truth
Lady Peace	The Shoes of the Gospel of Peace
Lady Justice (Righteousness)	The Breastplate of Righteousness

It became evident that this anonymous poet of the Middle Ages had made a connection that Paul had done before him. Fair enough, then. That would have been sufficient reason in the Middle Ages to yoke the two together.

However, I'd spent so long puzzling over why the Armour of God was connected to the kiss of the Four Daughters of God that the discovery Paul had already linked the two didn't really satisfy my curiosity. I'd found out why my favourite poet had done it but I was left with the question: *so why did Paul do it?*

He could have absolutely picked anything for those pieces of armour. They could have been similar to the fruits of the Spirit. Or the gifts of the Spirit. So why did the Holy Spirit inspire him to choose elements which evoked Psalm 85:10?

What has that kiss got to do with putting on armour?

Recall that in the Hebrew understanding of the Scriptures, there are four separate levels of interpretation.

- **Pashat** = *plain*, the obvious and surface meaning.

- **Remez** = *hint*, the deeper meaning; just beyond the literal.
- **Derash** = *inquiry*, the comparative, sifted meaning.
- **Sod** = *secret*, the meaning given through inspiration or revelation.

Paul has dropped a huge hint. He's given us a remez of the highest order.

The connection he has made between kissing and putting on armour is not insignificant, random, trivial or unimportant. If we get his hint, it's going to affect our understanding of spiritual warfare in his writing from several paragraphs back—beyond even 'Wives, submit to your husbands.'

The fact is that Paul didn't change the topic abruptly after his admonitions about marriage, children and slaves. Instead, he was summing up his teaching on nasa'—which extends all the way through to this passage—with a related concept: נשׁק, nashaq, meaning *to put on armour* but also meaning *to kiss* and *to kindle*.

It's a single interconnected line of thought: nasa' to nashaq. Because nashaq has a sense of both *armour* and *kiss*, the elements of God's panoply naturally evoke the warrior overtones in Rabbi Simon's contemporary story as well as the reconciling kiss of Mercy, Truth, Peace and Righteousness mentioned by the psalmist.

Put on the armour of God, Paul says in Ephesians 6:13.

Another equally valid way of expressing the idea behind his words is this: *Lift your face for the kiss of God.*

Isn't that just a sublime thought? Isn't it just a unique and utterly delectable concept?

God armours us when we turn to Him for a kiss.

The Lord bless you and keep you; the Lord make His face shine upon

God's Panoply

you, and be gracious to you; the Lord lift up His countenance upon you, and give you peace. So they shall put My name on the children of Israel, and I will bless them.

Numbers 6:24–27 NKJV

Ben was home alone with his little sister Sally when he decided to paint her portrait. His mother was shopping when he found some bottles of coloured ink and set diligently to work. Soon stains were everywhere—blots squiggled their way across the floor and a trail of smudges followed his progress along the furniture.

When his mother returned, she surveyed the mess in silence. She said nothing until she spotted the picture. 'Why, it's Sally!' she exclaimed, picking it up.

She kissed him.

'My mother's kiss made me a painter,' recalled Benjamin West.

He was to go on to become one of the most celebrated artists of the eighteenth century.

There is a loftier ambition than merely to stand high in the world. It is to stoop down and lift mankind a little higher.

Henry Van Dyke

For several days each week, I have a part-time job as a copy editor. One of the regular aspects of this job is to work on the Australian edition of the devotional *The Word for Today*.

On one occasion the daily reading made reference to a story by James Dobson about a friend of his. The friend had been going through a time of extreme financial stress. He became very angry one Christmas Eve with his three-year old daughter for wasting some gold wrapping paper. She'd tried to cover a box she'd found under the Christmas tree but had made a mess.

Next day she came to him with the same box and said it was for him. At this point, he became upset he'd over-reacted the previous day. Then his temper got the better of him again when he opened the box to find it empty.

He yelled at her that you don't give someone a present unless there's actually something inside. You don't give an empty box.

Tears in her eyes, the little girl said, 'Daddy, it's not empty. I blew kisses into it. I filled it with my love.'

The man was devastated.

He hugged his daughter and asked for her forgiveness. For years, he kept the gold-wrapped box by his bed and, whenever he felt especially low, he'd open it up and take out one of the imaginary kisses inside.

I thought this was an especially lovely story. It didn't say explicitly that kisses armour us against the hurts of life, but it was implicit.

I felt vaguely regretful that, before he died, I'd never thought to give my dad a gold-wrapped box full of kisses to show him my love. So I thought I should do it for my mum.

Not long afterwards, while doing my Christmas shopping, I saw a finely-spun glass bottle with a cork in the top designed to put in messages of love. Just the thing!

As my siblings, their spouses and their children arrived for a family Christmas celebration, I waylaid them, gave them a tiny piece of paper and a pen, and insisted they write something appropriate for my mum on it.

She had a wonderful time a few days later extracting the tiny rolled-up scrolls from the message bottle and reading them.

She was also able to respond to some of the messages in ways that ultimately changed the lives of the people involved.

Isn't it just so mysterious and wonderful the way nasa' works?

Long ago, a little girl wrapped up a gold box full of kisses. In the long chain of uplift, she's still making an impact and changing lives.

Therefore put on the full armour of God... Stand[64] firm then, with the belt of truth buckled around your waist, with the breastplate of righteousness in place, and with your feet[65] fitted[66] with the readiness[67] that comes from the gospel of peace. In addition... take up the shield[68] of faith, with which you can extinguish all the flaming arrows[69] of the evil one. Take the helmet of salvation and the sword of the Spirit, which is the word of God. And pray in the Spirit on all occasions with all kinds of prayers and requests. With this in mind, be alert and always keep on praying for all the saints.

Ephesians 6:13–18 NIV

Armour and kiss: the very same word in Hebrew? The very same concept?!

It seems almost incomprehensible.

Oops! I'd better be careful. I once got so excited about the armour of God in Ephesians 6 being identical to a divine kiss that I tumbled over my words and said just that.

An alert man picked me up sternly on my lack of rigorous thinking and told me I was entirely incorrect in this 'analysis'. Forget 'exegesis'; he wouldn't dignify my inane ramblings with that name. His problem with what I'd said? The Hebrew word *nashaq* does not mean *armour* or *kiss*—rather it means *to put on armour* or *to kiss*. It's a verb, not a noun.

I take his point. After all, as I said right at the start, in the language of heaven love is a verb. It is not a noun.

However, the sublime beauty of the idea—that God armours us by kissing us—that affection is protection—that love covers us against all manner of attack—simply eluded him.

His careful rationalist thinking couldn't take a slight inaccuracy in its stride. His mind was like one of the most impregnable fortresses of Arthurian literature: guarded by a bridge of razor-edged swords,[70] ready to slice word from meaning if it failed to conform to a precise definition.

He didn't understand my enthusiasm. I didn't understand his pedantry.

Almost without exception, Christian translations of the closing verses of Psalm 2 call on earthly kings to 'kiss the Son'. However, Jewish translations of *nashequ–bar* in Psalm 2:12 are not so consistent. 'Arm yourselves with purity' is the alternative they offer us.
Which is right? Is

- 'Kiss the Son, lest He be angry and you be destroyed in your way, for His wrath can flare up in a moment. Blessed are all who take refuge in Him.'

  more correct than

- 'Arm yourselves with purity lest He become angry and you perish in the way, for in a moment His wrath will be kindled;

the praises of all who take refuge in Him.'[71]

May I suggest they are as valid as each other? In the culture of the ancient Near East, a kiss was symbolic of submission.[72] It is for this reason the New Revised Standard Version translates this verse with 'kiss his feet' (although no feet are mentioned) since that is the one of the few English expressions which actually uses the word 'kiss' with a sense of submission. The New Living Translation on the other hand omits both 'kiss' and 'arm' with its offering: *Submit to God's royal son.*

However, as we have seen, our modern notions of 'submit' may not be altogether applicable. The Jewish translation hints at this in a way none of the Christian ones do: if by 'submit' we should be thinking 'lift up', then submission to God means lifting up His name. The well-attested way to do that is sing His praise.

Surely this is why Paul in Ephesians 5 turns immediately from his admonition in verses 19 and 20 to continually sing and make melody to the Lord in your heart, addressing each other in psalms and hymns and spiritual songs, to verse 22: *'Wives, submit to your husbands.'*

Because he was already discussing how we should be subject to God—by constant lifting up—it was perfectly natural for him to turn to how to be subject to one another.

And there's a very good reason why he'd start with wives rather than husbands in this discourse on mutuality. Because the word for 'wives' in Aramaic, a language Paul himself would have used, is *nasiyn.*[73]

Like stars sprinkled in the heavens, words evocative of *lifting up* sparkle all the way through this long section.

Surely this theme is why Paul book-ends his discussion of submission and armour—a topic running all the way from Ephesians 5:21 to 6:17—with similar thoughts: pray and offer praise in the Spirit.[74] He begins and ends with the same idea: lift up the name of God.

Indeed, it's almost as if he used the structure of a Hebrew poem—the concentric ring-structure which starts and finishes with the same concept. The outer ring refers to prayer and praise, the inner ring to armour-bearing and armour, the core to loving relationships with children and servants.

Like Jesus Himself, Paul latched on to *nasa'* and never let go.

So He said to them, 'When you lift up the Son of Man, you will know that "I Am Who I Am"; then you will know that I do nothing on My own authority, but I say only what the Father has instructed Me to say.'

John 8:28 GNT

Bear with me. Or skip the next few sections if you're one of those people convinced that, to understand Hebrew words, it's all about the letters. If, to you, the idea that the sound of the word itself or its component syllables should be taken into account is anathema, then pass over this part. I personally find sounds, particularly those which might be considered part of the poetry of the whole, to be fascinating and underrated. Many of the prophets used rhymes and assonances extensively as they warned of what was to come. The destiny of many towns was spelled out, not in the meaning of their names but rather in the meaning of words that rhymed with their names.

Consequently, I feel it is rewarding to look at a very interesting tail-rhyme.

Nashaq means *to put on armour* or *to kiss*.

Hashaq means *to be attached to* or *to love*.[75]

It has a sense of heart-to-heart connection—oneness, again!— desire and longing, heart's delight, love that is purposed and fixed.

It is used in Deuteronomy 7:7, Psalm 91:14 and Isaiah 38:17 to describe God's love for His people.[76] It tells us that God delights in us, yearns for our company and desires to be knitted as one with us.

The Lord your God is with you, He is mighty to save. He will take great delight in you, He will quiet you with His love, He will rejoice over you with singing.

Zephaniah 3:17 NIV

We are God's poem,[77] God's song, God's breath, God's infilled name, God's delight, the apple of His eye.

When we fell over as kids, we'd run to our mums and, more often than not, they'd kiss the hurt better. Off we'd go, running and tumbling again.

To God, the worst disease is curable by His kiss. So why doesn't it happen? Because we run to everybody and everything else first. We have so many false refuges in disappointment, so many hiding places where we lick our wounds—and often we don't even realise we're not going to God. There are dark covenants we've bought into—we may not have taken them out, but like the good kings of Israel who did not destroy the high places, we are complicit with their continuation.

It's often said that, for a little kid, love is spelt t–i–m–e.

That's true for more than kids. It's true for God. God constantly desires to spend time with us. That's how He wants to show us His love. But we, too busy to enjoy union and communion with Him, miss out on His kiss. And then we're not armoured for the slings and arrows of daily life.

Although God sings over us, He wants us to join in the singing. He wants us to swell the chorus of love that restores the universe.

At the end of his letter to the Ephesians, Paul mentions the

- Breastplate of righteousness
- Helmet of salvation
- Shoes of the preparation of the gospel of peace

- Belt of truth
- Shield of faith
- Sword of the word of God

Six pieces of armour.

Impossible! I didn't believe it for a moment. Paul—a Platonist? A number-adoring pro-Pythagorean Gnostic? There must be some mistake! A man circumcised on the eighth day, of the people of Israel, the tribe of Benjamin, a Hebrew of Hebrews[78] does not choose six with all its Greek cultural overtones when he could choose seven.

Religiously, the number six points to the Pythagoreans, particularly if it's in combination with 101. And there do happen to be 101 Greek words from Ephesians 6:13–18. Not to mention that 202-word sentence at the beginning of the letter.

There are particular numbers favoured by the Pythagoreans and thus by the Gnostics: these are 6, 16, 36 and especially 216, their number of re-incarnation.[79] The number 10 was massively important to them too, but the sixes were almost a signature. So much of a signature that Paul has to again fall under suspicion because of the oft-quoted fact that the theme of his letter to the Philippians is clearly 'joy' since he uses *chara* 16 times. Actually, this misses a word for 'joy' based on *kauchaomai*,[80] so Paul actually makes 17 references to it.

The world is back on its axis. I'm happy now. As my favourite writer—the author of *Sir Gawain and the Green Knight*—would have been. He too was anti-Platonist to the highest level. You see, there's one number the Pythagoreans would never use. One number they considered an 'atrocity' or 'abomination'.

It was 17.

Now whether this term came about because the apostles used 17 relentlessly (*How many things are unable to separate us from the love of God? How many times is 'Father' mentioned in the Sermon on the Mount? How many times does Matthew refer to Christ in his gospel? How many qualities are desirable for an elder? How often does Paul use sophia, wisdom, in his first letter to the Corinthians?*— and this is just the tip of the tip of the iceberg) or whether the apostles used it because they knew the Gnostics hated it, is besides the point. [81]

Somewhere in the description of the armour of God there should be a 17 lurking. And it would make much more sense if there were seven pieces of armour.

Of course there are.

The seventh piece is 'prayer': *pray at all times in the Spirit.*

It harks back to the psalms and hymns and spiritual songs of Ephesians 5:19. The perfect mirror endpapers for the sequence of thought: *nasiyn, nasa', nasu, hashequ, nashequ.*

But now it's imperative to find that missing 17.

Because, if I read the author of *Sir Gawain and the Green Knight* correctly, an allusion to singing in combinations of 101 words indicates worship of an entirely different messiah: Pythagoras.

Yes, you may recognise his name as that of an ancient mathematician who had a theorem about a right-angled triangle. It might seem surprising but the guy who made your life difficult in junior high school, where you had to learn that the square on the hypotenuse was equal to the sum of the squares on the other two sides, was worshipped as divine.

The influence of Pythagoras is under-estimated in our time. Every time neo-Platonism has resurged over the last two millennia it has had a Pythagorean component, comprised on the one hand of sacred mathematics and, on the other, of magic.

This is a battle of attrition and, at the moment, Christianity is in a period of long defeat. In fully embracing Greek thinking, our inheritance has been lost.

There's a tendency in many quarters to blame the Roman emperor Constantine for compromising Christianity when it became a state religion in the fourth century. The pressure to conform meant many people chose Christianity for reasons of convenience, rather than conscience. This view of history ignores what happened immediately after Constantine's death.

One of the all-time great promoters of Pythagoras emerged. Julian was Constantine's nephew and, after a season of considerable turmoil, he eventually assumed one of the thrones in a divided empire. Although he had been brought up as a Christian, Julian had turned to Pythagorean theurgy under the influence of Maximus of Ephesus, a student of Iamblichus.

He resolved to replace Christianity with neo-Platonic paganism. However, he was apparently of the opinion his uncle Constantine had done little more than bow to the wishes of the Empire as Christianity was the people's choice. Women, children and slaves actually liked being treated better than possessions. So, in his view, an imperial decree was not going to get rid of it. In fact, trying to halt the march of Christianity might be counter-productive.

What was lacking in Julian's estimation was a moral philosophy to rival the Christian ethical code. So he sent to the oracle of Delphi for advice. He also promoted the writings of Iamblichus, particularly *On the Pythagorean Life*, as the ethical basis of a return to paganism.

The Pythia—the last priestess of Delphi—reputedly delivered the oracle's final message:

Tell to the king that the carven hall is fallen in decay;
Apollo has no chapel left, no prophesying bay,
No talking spring. The stream is dry that had so much to say. [82]

Julian's short reign did much to ensure the fame of the catechism, *On the Pythagorean Life*. One of its questions referred to the oracle at Delphi and to Python Apollo, the tutelary deity after whom Pythagoras was named.

Question: What is the oracle of Delphi?

Answer: The tetraktys. It is also the harmony in which the Sirens sing.
This answer doesn't mean much today.

It's baffling and obscure.

But to Paul of Tarsus, John the Apostle and the author of *Sir Gawain and the Green Knight*, it would have been reason enough to whip out their mathematical knives and start some serious surgery.

The tetraktys (or tetract) was the ultimate mystical symbol of Pythagoreans: it was simply 10 dots arranged in a triangle.

The Pythagoreans worshipped it: they regarded it as Manifest Deity, the source of nature, the Number of Numbers, the Meaning of Meaning, the creative principle, the fundamental Truth of the universe, the heart of the Logos.

And by Logos, they definitely did not mean Jesus of Nazareth. Unless they happened also to be Gnostic Christians who tried to fuse the two ideas and view Jesus as the re-incarnation of Pythagoras who had been dead some five hundred years.

Hidden in this enigmatic answer from *On the Pythagorean Life* is a claim that Pythagoras (in his guise as Python Apollo or Hyperborean Apollo) is the creator and sustainer of the cosmos.

Creator: because, as far as the Pythagoreans were concerned, numbers (which then were also alphabetic letters) were the essence of creation. This is not far from Hebrew belief—except of course for the suggestion that Yahweh and Python Apollo were equivalent.

Sustainer: the Sirens were each supposed to sing one note of the musical scale. However, creating a perfect octave on a stringed instrument is not simply a matter of doubling the length of the string. There is a tiny difference in size, equivalent to just over 101% and which today is called a 'Pythagorean comma' or 'diatonic comma'.

During the Middle Ages, this miniscule percentage over and

above the whole was apparently regarded as the way God sustained the universe via the Music of the Spheres. It was the angel's portion. Or the siren's portion. Depending on which side of the divide—Christian or Platonic—you fell.[83]

This, I'm certain, is what the 101 refers to in the work of the author of *Sir Gawain and the Green Knight*: directly to the Music of the Spheres and indirectly to God as sustainer of the universe.

This, I also believe, is probably what Paul is saying by his use of 202 words at the beginning of Ephesians and 101 words within the Armour of God sequence in Ephesians 6:13–18. The fact is, Paul actually starts his 202-word sentence by alluding to God the creator and sustainer.

This cannot be coincidence. He's making a point about Delphi. It's a subtle one—but I have little doubt readers at the time would have got it.

The reason I'm harping on about this so much is that it's not really about the numbers: it's about what they signify. More and more, as I am involved in prayer counselling for people who are unable to cross the threshold into their destiny, I find they have repeatedly lost a battle with an enemy they don't even know exists: Python—the spirit of the Delphic Oracle.

Remember again that there are four separate levels of interpretation in the Hebrew understanding of the Scriptures.

- **Pashat** = *plain*, the obvious and surface meaning.
- **Remez** = *hint*, the deeper meaning; just beyond the literal.
- **Derash** = *inquiry*, the comparative, sifted meaning.
- **Sod** = *secret*, the meaning given through inspiration or revelation.

In Paul's sequence about the Armour of God, the *pashat* level is simply about Roman armour and the protection it offers the wearer.

Although I have suggested that the kiss of mercy, truth, righteousness and peace is the *remez* level, I'm going to now point out it is probably meant to be the *derash*.

The *remez*—just beyond the literal—can only be penetrated once we realise that Paul has carefully chosen a set of Greek words with inspired double meanings.

The word he used for 'shield' is also a word for *door*.

The word he used for 'darts' is also a word for *threshold*.

The word he used for 'stand' comes from words for *pillars* or *doorposts*.

The connotation of helmet could be *lintel*. And he mentions *shoes*.

Quite simply, there is a series of puns referring to a threshold covenant, the most obscure major covenant of ancient times. In addition, the use of 101 alludes to one of the threshold guardians—Python, the spirit of constriction, who obstructs the doorway into destiny.

What protects us against Delphic Python?

Paul never made any secret of that. He'd said it before and he's just spelled it out again and again: covenantal, armour-bearing love.

That they may be one, Father, just as You are in Me and I am in You. May they also be in Us so that the world may believe...

John 17:21 NIV

A threshold covenant is a very complex matter. To deal with one, if it is operational in your life, is not simple. It requires unusual persistence and faith.

The next book in this series will explore the issue of problematic threshold covenants and how to deal with them. But first, it's important to establish in your mind what a true godly covenant is. Without that understanding, it's impossible to recognise what's gone wrong.

Before we go on, I'd like to go a little deeper with the armour of God. It's not really into the *sod*—secret—layer because anyone 2000 years ago would have spotted this immediately. Still, I'm a bit reluctant to go there because this is the boundary between mathematics and the occult: gematria.

However it's worth noting the words of Ronald Youngblood: *'Flagrant abuse of various forms of numerology, including especially gematria, should not be permitted to blind us to the undoubted use of numbers in a figurative sense or of numbers as a literary device in the Bible (as well as elsewhere in the ancient world.)'*

So, with due caution, let's venture into that world where alpha equals one, beta equals two and so on.

When I was considering the possibility the Armour of God refers to a covenant, I realised I couldn't truly be sure this was the case unless there was a multiple of 111 or 1111 or 11111 somewhere in the design.

Strings-of-one are emblematic in medieval literature of either covenant or the kiss of heaven and earth. Just to prove the poets of the Middle Ages didn't devise this idea themselves, 111 is found as a structural device in the seventeenth chapter of John's gospel. Maarten Menken in *Numerical Literary Techniques in John—The Fourth Evangelist's Use of Numbers of Words and Syllables* points out its repeated use there. (Perhaps there are other places it occurs, too—I went straight to Menken's analysis of John 17 on the basis that, if 111 or 1111 as a mathematical metaphor for covenant occurred anywhere, that was the first place to look. I was so delighted at finding it I didn't search any further.)

From this, I developed my hypothesis. There were seven pieces of armour if the songs of praise are counted as the last piece. Therefore, if the gematria of Ephesians 6:12–18 referred to *covenant*, it should be 77777.

To my dismay when I added it up, it wasn't.

It's 77791.

To be so close was upsetting beyond belief. My background is science and I know that, in terms of error, 14 in 77777 is so small as to be negligible in Greek thinking.

In Hebrew thinking, however, my allowed margin of error is 1. That's the most I'll ever get.

So 77791, close as it was to 77777, wasn't nearly close enough.

My Greek isn't good at all. Certainly not good enough to check for possible error in the text I was consulting. I was getting into a dark broody mood when I thought I heard God speak: 'You know, if this were a medieval text, you wouldn't be scowling over it like this. You'd have already divided that number and the ones either side of it by 17 and 22.'

I immediately whipped out my calculator. Incredibly, 77792 is divisible by 17, 22, 52 and 4.

In my research I'd come across lots of medieval poetry built on 17 or 22 but I'd never previously encountered anything that had both! I was thrilled.

The special aspect of 77792 is that it's close enough to 77777 to indicate *covenant*. However, it has that all-important 17—the numerical motif of the early Christians—built explicitly into it. It also has 22, so significant to the Jews because it was the number of letters in their alphabet. In addition it has 52, which I presume is a motif of *time*, being the number of weeks in a year, as well as 4 for a motif of *space*: the four corners of the earth.

And it's got 101 words.

Thus the total metaphor refers to *sustaining covenant armour*. According to the encoded mathematics, it protects the wearer at all times, in all places and is proof against the principalities and powers of a threshold and, no doubt, whatever seals and curses might be spoken over the doorway.

It's a mathematical design incredibly similar to that used by the author of *Sir Gawain and the Green Knight* in his four poem sequence (which also includes *Pearl, Purity* and *Patience*). And I wouldn't have had a clue what Paul was saying without the hints that medieval poet was gracious enough to drop everywhere.

Neo-platonism, especially with its Pythagorean yoke, is the most ancient enemy of Christianity. Thomas Merton called Platonism a sin.

In *The Seven Storey Mountain*, he wrote that he would be filled with suppressed indignation whenever phrases like 'the Good, the True, and the Beautiful' came up. Such wording became a code for the sin of Platonism, reducing reality to a purely abstract level and viewing it as a mere shadow of a remote ideal. Reality was an essence that seemed to be filed away in a heavenly card-index while godlings milled around the Logos expressing their excitement in high, fluted tones, redolent of English intellectualism.

I really relate to Merton's sentiment.

I seethe when people try to convince me simple beauty, unadorned truth and natural goodness in literature will lead readers to Christ. When people are ignorant of Platonism they don't realise 'the Good, the True and the Beautiful' doesn't do anything of the kind. Instead of the concrete uplift of covenantal oneness, it can lead up, up and away into lofty, exalted abstraction—an entirely different Logos than Jesus of Nazareth.

There's always a choice.

Even virtues have their dark side.

I didn't know this until I came to look into the meaning of the name Melissa. I tell part of the story in *God's Poetry*:

> *I was reading a draft of a story by my friend, Melissa, when I was suddenly struck by the prevalence of symbols for ash trees in her story. There weren't*

any actual ash trees, just symbols of them. Could it be, I wondered, that there was some connection to her name? A check of over two dozen books listed only two possibilities: honey or bee. Nothing else. No ash tree. No tree of any kind, in fact.

If I hadn't encountered the vague clue from Melissa's writing, I would never have suspected anything else. Yet if you check ash tree itself, it transpires that way back in classical Greece, Melissa really did start life as meaning ash tree. Just to complicate matters, you'll find that sometimes the North Pole is referred to poetically as a melissa.

How can a tree become a bee? Let alone the North Pole?

The process was a very long one. It transpires the name of the nymph of the mountain ash tree was originally Melias. A nymph was an elemental spirit, not quite in the league of a goddess; a dryad whose life was tied to the ash tree. In time, Melias came to refer not to the nymph but to the ash tree itself. Then it came to be the name of the secretion of the ash tree—a sweet substance also known as manna. As centuries passed, the sense of the word changed again from the manna produced by the tree to any sweet ambrosial food. When ambrosia—the food of the gods—came to mean a mead-like fermented drink, its sense shifted subtly again. Eventually, Melissa came to refer to the honey from which the mead was produced, then to the bee that produced the honey.

Meantime, over the two thousand years this

123

particular series of changes was occurring, a second stream of meaning was also taking place. Melias— the nymph of the ash tree—became, by natural association, the ash tree itself. The ash tree also became a symbol of a hallowed place at the sacred centre of the land: three of the five sacred trees of Ireland were ash trees and so too was Yggdrasil, the World Ash Tree of Norse mythology, the axis of all the nine realms of gods, men and giants.

It's a short distance from the concept of a central world axis to the notion of the North Pole and this would appear to be how Melissa came to be a poetic name for it.

What I had left out of this story was how Melissa and I came to be friends. She had really loved a story I'd written and asked me to help her with her own writing. As I looked back on my story, I suddenly realised why she'd liked it so much: symbols of the North Pole pervaded it. In the light of her name, it made perfect sense.

But I was baffled. None of my polar symbols were intentional. Not one of them. I sat down and I did something I often do: I interrogate my own writing to see what God is telling me through it. 'What on earth,' I asked Him, 'is a Tyrian cynosure? Because that's what I've got here. It's more than the North Pole, it's a cynosure.'

'A cynosure is exactly what the dictionary says: a guiding light,' He replied. 'And Tyrian refers to honour, integrity and fidelity.'

'Well, that makes sense. Those are the things I value most in life. Those are the things I sacrifice for.'

'Yes, indeed you do.'

'Why is the North Pole like a Tyrian cynosure?'

'There are two North Poles: geographic and magnetic,' He pointed out. 'If you start out for the geographic North using a compass, it will be a considerable time before your direction starts to be seriously amiss.'

'You're telling me I'm off-track with You? I'm telling myself through what I've written that I'm off-track with You? How?'

'Honour, integrity and fidelity are part of My character. They are not Me. It is a very subtle error to worship aspects of My character, and to separate them from Me.'

For me, honour, integrity and fidelity were my own private version of 'the Good, the True and the Beautiful'. I had to take them to the cross and crucify them. That was hard. But virtues as they were, they'd become sin. They'd become more important to me than God himself. I finally knew that when He asked, 'Are you willing to give them up?' and my first thought was, 'I'd rather die!'

A Tyrian cynosure is like Nehushtan, the bronze serpent Moses lifted up in the wilderness to bring healing to the people. Hezekiah had to destroy it because it had become an idol.

Just so, virtues can become idols.

The fact is, I coped with God's paradoxical nature by picking and mixing the aspects I liked and emulating them. But copying is not oneness.

It was only as I fell into that carefully-laid trap the day my class came up the stairs chanting doggerel and, as a consequence, started to explore medieval poetry I began to realise likeness and oneness weren't necessarily the same.

The past has so much to teach us.

We have lost our spiritual heritage and the treasures of knowledge our ancestors fought to preserve for us.

Sometimes a light surprises
the child of God who sings;
it is the Lord who rises

healing in his wings;
when comforts are declining
he grants the soul again
a season of clear shining
to cheer it after rain.

William Cowper

If my class hadn't annoyed me so much that day, I wouldn't have investigated the research of Joan Helm. And fortunately I wasn't able to find the particular work of hers I wanted easily. So I had to make do with *Eric and Enide: Cosmic Measures in Nature and the Hebrew Heritage*, where she discusses Chrétien de Troyes' poem *Eric and Enide* and land measurement. At the same time, I examined the poems in the manuscript where *Sir Gawain and the Green Knight* occurs.

I noticed the same unusual numbers in both. By unusual I mean 176, 1056 and 1743. Joan Helm equated these numbers with an esoteric idea: the kiss of the earth and the moon. It was a neo-Platonic version of the marriage of heaven and earth.

I couldn't imagine the author of *Sir Gawain and the Green Knight*, anti-Platonist as he was with all his structural seventeens, being able to stomach this. Especially given the highly dubious Christianity of some other poems by Chrétien de Troyes.[84] So I asked myself: 'What would be a Christian response to this? What would the kiss of heaven and earth look like to a Christian of the Middle Ages?'

I decided the answer had to be the only kiss I could think of —that in Psalm 85:10. This was long before I discovered the connection in Hebrew between *kissing* and *putting on armour*. All I knew was, if I was correct, then on a particular line in the manuscript's third poem, I would find a reference to Psalm 85.

God's Panoply

At first sight, it didn't look like it. Fortunately a footnote explained that the line in question and those around it were probably references to the Debate of the Four Daughters of God. Although this didn't sound promising, it transpired this was exactly what I was looking for. The whole concept of the Four Daughters of God revolved around Psalm 85:10–11.

I was so elated by my success, I began to predict what would be on exact lines of the various poems. Mainly, with astonishing success.

I want to step back now into Joan Helm's work. Although she did not mention Psalm 85, she uncovered where its idea of the string-of-ones originated. This is so lovely a concept that, even if you are not mathematically minded, please stay the distance.

Now mathematics is full of fascinating curiosities. I agree with the Platonists on some things. Mathematics, for me, is discovered, not invented: it is part of God's created order, not part of humanity's achievements. There are many mathematicians who hold a contrary view.

This aside, let's turn to the number 12345679 (note 8 is missing). Multiply it by 8 and it turns into 98765432. Play with it some more and:

$$12345679 \times 9 = 111111111$$
$$12345679 \times 18 = 222222222$$
$$12345679 \times 27 = 333333333$$
$$12345679 \times 36 = 444444444$$
$$12345679 \times 45 = 555555555$$
$$12345679 \times 54 = 666666666$$
$$12345679 \times 63 = 777777777$$
$$12345679 \times 72 = 888888888$$
$$12345679 \times 81 = 999999999$$

Now, take the very last number and multiply it by the very first number and (drum roll, please!):

$$12345679 \times 999999999 = 111111111 \times 111111111$$
$$= 12345678987654321$$

That last number is truly the alpha to omega of the world of mathematics and, until I discovered it in Joan Helm's analysis of *Erec and Enide*, I'd always thought of it as lovely but ultimately useless. I'd used it to awe a few 12 year old boys in my time, but that always seemed to be the limit of its practicality.

Yes, it's true—I confess. I used to be a Greek thinker.

The late Chinese politician, Chou En-Lai, was once asked by a reporter what he thought the effect of the French Revolution had been on history. His reply is legendary: 'It's too early to tell.'

In mathematics, however, it's a different story: the effect of the French Revolution is abundantly clear. It brought us the decimal system of measurement.

In Australia, we don't have yards any longer, we have metres; we don't have miles, we have kilometres; we don't have acres, we have hectares.

This is a vastly simplified system, but the previous one has never been completely overturned. It hasn't quite been erased from people's minds even after nearly 50 years of use in Australia. Fabric shops tend to be a preserve of inches and yards. While the new system might be a massive simplification of the old, be assured it's no easier to learn. I have regularly *tried* to teach classes of sixteen-year-olds the metric system but they still get confused by whether there are ten millimetres in a centimetre or a hundred.

The architects of the French Revolution were not, in fact, wanting to simplify an archaic system when they gave orders for the devising of a new measurement system. They were intent on taking God out of the picture—out of society, out of history and indeed, even out of measurement itself.

Now I'd never really thought of God as intimately connected with measurement but that only goes to show how much I'd been influenced by our culture.

The French knew better. Chrétien de Troyes tried to warp measurement out of its Hebrew grounding and give it a Platonic

God's Panoply

spin. The revolutionaries of the late eighteenth century took it a step further. Instead of 12 inches in a foot and 3 feet in a yard and 1760 yards in a mile, everything became multiples of 10. They even tried to make a week of 10 days, but that didn't last very long at all. It turned out the human body actually needs a rest every 7 days.

These ardent atheists two centuries back were responsible for getting rid of the following system which they believed was full of references to God.

12 lines = 1 inch

12 inches = 1 foot (=144 lines)

3 feet = 1 yard

22 yards = 1 chain

10 chains = 1 furlong (= 40 poles)

8 furlongs = 1 mile (=1760 yards)

Now, despite always knowing the metric system was essentially anti-Christian in inspiration, it never really occurred to me that the French were attacking anything of true significance. Those numbers— 3, 10, 12, 22, 40, 144 and 1760—were so messy, complicated and apparently random, I couldn't see what they were thinking.

It didn't occur to me until Joan Helm made it clear that there isn't anything haphazard about those numbers. They are not the result of cobbling together different systems from all over, but are carefully and wonderfully thought out.

At some time during the Dark Ages, someone unknown chose them to reflect not only the important recurring numbers in Scripture but designed them so that the seemingly bizarre measurement, the acre, mirrored Ezekiel's vision of the City of God: the City of Yahweh Shammah (*'The Lord Is There'*) outlined in chapter 48.

- 3—Trinity
- 10—Commandments
- 12—Apostles
- 22—Number of letters in the Hebrew alphabet (and, for the Jews, the number of books in Scripture; for both Christians and

Jews, in medieval times 22 was considered to be the number of different types of things God created at the beginning of Genesis, thus it signified 'completeness in creation'—the idea of 7 as signifying 'completion' is a recent one)

- 40—the number of years the Israelites wandered in the wilderness and the number of days Jesus spent in the desert
- 144—recalls the 144,000 elect in the book of Revelation

There's only one unexplained number. Where does 1760 come from?

It's very simple. Today we think that the ancient measure called a 'cubit' varied according to the length of a person's arm. Medieval people believed differently. They thought a cubit was exactly 17.6 inches. They applied this understanding to the City of God in Ezekiel's vision.

In Ezekiel 48, the City of God is described as 18000 cubits in perimeter. Since it's a square, this means each side is 4500 cubits. 4500 cubits at 17.6 inches per cubit is 79200 inches (or 6600 feet or 2200 yards or 100 chains).

In fact, it's precisely and exactly 1000 acres.

In fact, the acre—a truly bizarre land measure[85] for anyone to have come up with in the age before orbiting satellites—seems to have been designed precisely so that 1000 of them would equal the area of the City of God.

That City's suburbs extend, according to the description, another 250 cubits north, south, east and west. This means that the City of Yahweh Shammah including its suburbs is a square of side 5000 cubits.

Now here's the power of mathematics: it doesn't matter whether medieval people were right or wrong about the cubit being 17.6 inches. If you're looking for a ratio, it's not actually necessary to know the size of the cubit.

The *area* of the City with suburbs compared to *area* of the City without suburbs is 1.2345679,[86] that curious number missing an 8 which when multiplied by 999999999 produces the alpha to omega of the number world.

So, hidden in the numbers of the City of God seen by Ezekiel, there's an image of completeness in creation—a completeness in *new* creation, actually—which medieval people tried to symbolise in the way they measured their fields and commons and greens.

In addition, the *length* of the side of the City with its suburbs compared to that without is 5000:4500 or 1.111111111111... on to infinity.

Here's the string-of-ones. It signifies Yahweh Shammah, *the Lord is there.* From the beginning of Scripture, the string-of-ones has been emblematic of the City of God and covenantal faithfulness to Yahweh.

It's both overt and covert in the story of Melchizedek, king of Salem, to whom Abraham gave a tithe. It's in the gematria and in the concept of a tithe. If I have $1000000 and tithe to my church, they'd get $100000. If my church then tithed to missions, they'd get $10000. If they then tithed, it would be $1000. And so on. If everyone tithed, then the total value of the tithes would be $111111.11—again reflecting the string–of–ones.

Or we could forget about fractions entirely. It's an Egyptian concept, after all. We could go back to what both the Greeks and Hebrews were more comfortable with: the ratio. A tithe is 1 part for God, 9 parts for the giver.

In ratio terms, 1:9 = 0.11111...

A heavenly number!

These shall be its measurements: the north side 4500 cubits, the south side 4500 cubits, the east side 4500 cubits, and the west side 4500 cubits. The city shall have open spaces: on the north 250 cubits, on the south 250 cubits, on the east 250 cubits, and on the west 250 cubits.

Ezekiel 48:16–17 NAS

Like the Greek poet Isocrates who apologised for going outside the 'due measures', I'm going to apologise for failing to finish my thoughts for the last section in my allotted 'due measure' of 1743 words. Unlike Isocrates, who simply stopped his story dead on the spot, I'm going to go on now and explain where 1743 comes from.

Joan Helm noted 1742 as a significant number featured in *Eric and Enide*. I noted 1743 was also used in the manuscript of *Sir Gawain and the Green Knight*. It seemed unlikely this was a coincidence, since they both—in very different ways—feature a 'kiss of heaven and earth'.

She believed the number came from the inches in the perimeter of an acre (one chain wide by one furlong long): 17424 inches. It's simply a truncation of the first four digits.

Or: rather than a truncation, is it a tithe of 17424?

There's a tendency in many Christian circles today to say that to insist on tithing is legalistic. It's law, not grace. It's Old Testament, not New.

Tithing, however, is an expression of covenant faithfulness.

And it's an important expression of it because money is where so many of us go wrong.

For the people of the Middle Ages, the idea of the City of God was not an impossible ideal. They were incredibly serious about creating 'thin places' where heaven met earth. They wanted those places everywhere. Their obsession with 'squaring the circle' reflects this: consider a square inside a circle and the ratio of the perimeter to the circumference. Using their fractional approximations, they got 1.11133... I'm sure they thought if they could refine the fractions better, the divine 'heaven-kissing-earth' number would just pop out. In fact, it won't. You'll never get it, even with irrational numbers.

However, they didn't stop trying: tithing and the land measurement system with its acres reflecting the City of God were just a start in this regard.

And you could encode it in poetry:

- three collections of six different verse types totalling 6666 letters (the Gnomic poems of the Exeter book)
- one poem of 1212 lines with 101 repeated lines, making 1111 different lines (the great Middle English poem *Pearl* by the same author as *Sir Gawain and the Green Knight*)

...to name just two.

This was a world in which faith was so integrated into the fabric of life you couldn't go out and plough your acres without heaven impinging on your activity. You couldn't listen to such a poem being read without breathing in an atmosphere drenched with Yahweh Shammah, *the Lord is there.*

And all of this mathematical activity was so the City of God was immanent in the world.

Remember *nashamah*—God breathing life into us by whispering our names? Look closely at the word. Does it also encode besides shem, *name* and nasha, *bear* or *carry* or *lift up*, shammah for *God's immanence in both our names and our lives*?

Or, at least, that's what our lives should be about: God's immanence.

In *God's Poetry*, I show how name covenants are very often with gods we don't even know exist. Because covenants, as we have seen, are forever and follow family lines, we can often be affected by spiritual realities of which we are entirely ignorant: if a family or personal name has a dark dedication over it, this does not shift until it is renounced and re-dedicated. An obvious example of re-dedication is CS Lewis, famous for *The Lion, the Witch and the Wardrobe*. His surname comes from Llew, *lion*, the Celtic godling of light.

I should point out the one exception to the everlasting nature of covenants: the incredibly perverted covenant with Death which God specifically exempts from the rule.

One of my favourite books by Lewis is *The Silver Chair*. In it, he alludes to the Delphic Oracle and is most anti-Pythagorean in sentiment. It's almost enough to overlook his pro-Platonic lapse at the end of *The Last Battle*.

The subtlety of the references Lewis makes in *The Silver Chair* to Delphi match Paul's own subtlety. Two of the most famous passages in his epistles allude to Python: the Armour of God in Ephesians 6 and the Love Chapter in 1 Corinthians 13. In fact, there are many barely veiled allusions to the rites and practices of Delphi in the first letter to the Corinthians. This is not surprising since Delphi was just across the bay from Corinth.

Lewis, unlike Paul, gives us hints as to how this spirit operates. His green witch is modelled on the Pythia—the oracular priestess. When she turns into a huge green snake and wraps herself, python-like, around Prince Rilian, she reveals her true nature as a spirit of constriction. She's also modelled on the Lady of the Green Girdle in *Sir Gawain and the Green Knight* as her name 'The Lady of the Green Kirtle' hints. This is exceptionally appropriate as that author loathed the Pythagorean spirit emanating from Delphi with a passion—but was an even greater master of subtlety in alluding to it.

In Lewis' story, the heroes enter the witch's realm through a trench shaped like an E. This refers to the famous E engraved on the navelstone at Delphi. It was so ancient that, by the first century, no one knew its meaning. Though the famous suggestion of Plutarch was *if*, the ultimate word of choice and, so he maintained, of Python Apollo.

If I speak with the tongues of men and of angels...
If I have prophetic powers...
If I have all faith...
If I give away all I have...

Make no mistake about it, Paul was on the attack with these remarks. And his target was Delphi.

What does Lewis tell us about the way Python operates?

First prong of attack: memory. If you don't remember your sin, then how can you deal with it? If it dawns on you a spirit of constriction exists but you forget it straight away, how can you do anything about it?

Second prong of attack: doubt. Ok, you've got past forgetting. You've remembered. Now the doubts start. Is God really able to act? He never has before: you've never got past this threshold yet. Why would you be able to do it now?

Third prong of attack: constriction. Constriction of finances, circumstances, health... you name it and this spirit will try it.

If *all* that doesn't work, Python has a friend: the spirit of wasting. Not to mention several back-up plans.

So don't approach a threshold quickly.

Begin the long slow advance by asking Jesus to step into your name and become immanent there.

 נשׁא

The gematria of nasa', *lift off*, is not 110 or 111. However, as you might expect, there is an associated word which is: banner is *nec* in Hebrew and its gematria is 110. Thus Jehovah Nissi (Yahweh Nicci) has that sense of building up begun by a tithe. The string-of-ones is made of building blocks which are tithed tithes. But tithed tithes (the 'wave offering') are again simply an expression of mutuality and covenant faithfulness.

The blessing God promises for tithing is none other than that He has always pledged for faithfulness to His covenant. The blessing for working together is like Zion and Sion kissing: a lifting up and bestowal of everlasting life.

Like the eagle soaring, that lift-up is also to renew and revive. The word *eagle* in Hebrew is 'nesher'.

Its root is said to be an unused one, meaning *to lacerate*.

Permit me a doubt or two on this meaning. It's true an eagle tears and lacerates its prey but it also lifts its wings and soars. Nesher is not only far too much like nasa', its gematria is 550. The gematria increases to 555, however, for 'the eagle'.[87]

So nesher means *lacerate*? Hmmm... When we have a multiple of 110 for nec, *banner*? Or a multiple of 111, the simply sublime heaven-touching-earth number?

At this point, may I direct your attention to that historic day in 1969 when the first man stepped out on to the surface of the moon?

On July 16, NASA announced, 'We have lift-off,' as a Saturn V rocket left the launch–pad and Apollo XI began its journey to the moon.

Do you remember what, four days later, Neil Armstrong said as the lunar module touched down safely?

Do you know what Buzz Aldrin did immediately after landing?

God hides His fingerprints in the pages of history. However He doesn't hide them particularly well. They are so sticky with love and covenantal faithfulness, it's easy to find His passing in a string-of-ones left behind at the scene.

How good and pleasant it is when brothers live together in unity! It is like precious oil poured on the head, running down on the beard, running down on Aaron's beard, down upon the collar of his robes. It is as if the dew of Hermon [Sion] were falling on Mount Zion. For there the Lord bestows his blessing, even life forevermore.

Psalm 133 NIV

The first time Scripture mentions Melchizedek is when Abram—who was not yet Abraham—returns from battle. Five kings had rebelled against their overlord and, during the hostilities, Abram's nephew was taken captive. The brief but significant reference to Melchizedek occurs in Genesis 14:18–20.

Then Melchizedek king of Salem brought out bread and wine. He was priest of God Most High, and he blessed Abram, saying, 'Blessed be Abram by God Most High, Creator of heaven and earth. And blessed be God Most High, who delivered your enemies into your hand.' Then Abram gave him a tenth of everything.

Hints of a threshold covenant exist in these verses. Note that Abram then declares his allegiance to God with reference to *lifting up*:

The king of Sodom said to Abram, 'Give me the people and keep the goods for yourself.' But Abram said to the king of Sodom, 'I have raised my hand to the Lord, God Most High, Creator of heaven and earth, and have taken an oath that I will accept nothing belonging to you, not even a thread or the thong of a sandal, so that you will never be able to say, "I made Abram rich." I will accept nothing but what my men have eaten...'

Genesis 14:21–24 NIV

Following this renunciation of favour from anyone but God, the overture to a blood covenant begins:

After this, the word of the Lord came to Abram in a vision: 'Do not be afraid, Abram. I am your shield, your very great reward.' ...He took him outside and said, 'Look up at the heavens and count the stars—if indeed you can count them.' Then He said to him, 'So shall your offspring be.' Abram believed the Lord, and He credited it to him as righteousness.

Genesis 15:1, 5–6 NIV

God then initiates a covenant with Abram. During the name exchange, Abram becomes Abraham. He takes on the 'h' of HaShem, the Name, becoming the only man ever called the 'Friend of God'.

God becomes his covenant defender, in later generations re-affirming his covenant with his descendants Isaac and Jacob.

Note the progression leading up to the blood covenant:

- Threshold covenant including practical declaration of allegiance to God
- Renunciation of favour from other sources
- Personal promise from God and active faith in that promise

The holes in our covenant armour often result from what we have failed to renounce. We depend on the favour of the 'king of Sodom' but expect God to be our shield and very great reward anyway. We don't tithe, we don't make any practical expression of our covenant faithfulness. Moreover, by depending on the 'king of Sodom' we are actually being unfaithful.

By the curious thinking pervading our age, we think this doesn't matter.

God will remain faithful.

Because He cannot deny Himself.

It's the same sort of logic the people of Judah used to comfort themselves, before the Babylonian invasion.

'The Eagle has landed.'

Neil Armstrong, 20 July 1969

God's Panoply

Medieval people were serious about ensuring heaven kissed earth. As serious about it as the Psalmist was about Sion kissing Zion, north and south coming together as one, the heights of Hermon meeting the Temple mount.

The folk of the Middle Ages had it all worked out: if the moon came down so that its surface just brushed that of earth, then the circumference of the moon's orbit would be 31680 miles.[88] Until satellite mapping of the last few decades, this figure would prove to stand the test of time with stunning accuracy.

Now serendipitously, the perimeter of the City of God (that 1000 acre square) was 316800 inches.

This happy congruence of digits assumed even more importance according to Joan Helm because it so happened 3168 was also the numerological value of the Greek letters for Lord Jesus Christ, *Kurios Iesous Cristos*.[89]

It was all too perfect. Particularly since the common aspect of both 3168 and 1111 as theological symbols—mathematical metaphors for covenantal concepts—was the geometry of the City of God.

On 20 July 1969, the divide between the earth and the moon was conquered as the lunar module, the *Eagle*, landed on the Sea of Tranquillity.

The 'infernal' regions between the earth and the moon may not have collapsed to nothing, rolled up like a scroll, pursed together like a kiss or folded up into a neat spatial pleat, but the distance between the two was no longer an impassable barrier.

Just a few days after lift-off, moments after the *Eagle* landed, a covenant ceremony took place on the moon.

How appropriate our medieval ancestors would have thought such an event!

Although this ceremony was one of the very first acts to happen on the lunar surface, for many years it remained completely unknown to the general public.

Edwin 'Buzz' Aldrin was the co-pilot of Apollo 11 (of course, eleven, what else?) and the second person to step out onto the surface of the moon. He was an elder in his Presbyterian church at the time and carried with him a communion wafer and a vial of communion wine blessed by his pastor.

After the *Eagle* touched down, he read a portion of Scripture and took communion, after asking listeners on earth to give thanks in their own way.

'I am the vine, you are the branches. Whoever abides in Me will bring forth much fruit. Apart from Me you can do nothing.'

This verse he read from John 15:5 is the essence of covenantal oneness. As a vine cannot be separate from its branches, so anyone in covenant relationship with Christ can never be separate from Him.

Aldrin wanted his short ceremony to be broadcast back to earth. However NASA decided against it. The space agency was embroiled at the time in a lawsuit with well-known atheist Madalyn Murray O'Hair over a reading from the book of Genesis which had occurred the previous December while Apollo 8 was orbiting the moon.[90]

It was not until years later that Aldrin revealed his first action on reaching the Sea of Tranquillity.

Tranquillity.

A facet of peace.

One of the Four Daughters of God.

Indeed, the only Daughter whose name all modern commentators are agreed on. Indeed Apollo XI returned to earth on 24 July 1969—which happens to be 11118 days before the end of the century.[91]

It seems almost a tragedy that it's so close to 11111 days but not exactly matching it. However, I hope you've guessed that 11118 is the closest number to 11111 divisible by 17. The lunar landing itself was 11122 days from the end of the century: just one away from 11123, a number divisible by 49—a mathematical symbol of mercy and forgiveness.

If you think all this is just a curious 'coincidence' of history, try another: the Hubble Space telescope, sitting in that margin of space where medieval people would have said heaven touches earth, weighs 11110 kg.

And here's yet another: 11/11/11:00—each year at 11 a.m. on November 11, Armistice Day commemorates the declaration of peace at the end of World War I by 1 minute of silence.

And still another: the 'love song' of the Welsh revival was the hymn by the bard Gwilym Hiraethog (also known as William Rees) which ends:

> *Grace and love, like mighty rivers,*
> *Poured incessant from above,*
> *And heav'n's peace and perfect justice*
> *Kissed a guilty world in love.*

With an allusion like that to Psalm 85:10, there should be a string-of-ones hiding somewhere. By this time, you should have learned to suspect, as I have, that our covenant-keeping God keeps a light, almost invisible hand on history but, if you look closely, you'll find His fingerprints. The exact date when Welsh revival started is unknown. The best that can be ascertained is sometime in the fortnight after 31 October 1904.

Now it happens that this day—Halloween in many places—is traditionally the last day of the Celtic year. It also happens next day is 1/11 and ten days after that is 11/11, but these string-of-ones happen to occur every year, so there's nothing ultra-special about them.

Let's do some actual mathematical calculation. From the beginning of the century 01/01/01 to the last day of the fortnight after 31 October 1904 is a count of 1414 days. I love it! Medieval poets would surely tell me that, since the factors are 2, 7 and 101 that God has planned a celebration of Sabbath and song. (Or they might have considered it not by its factors but by its additive terms: the luscious combination of 1111+303 springs to mind.[92])

But how many days is it, not in the normal year, but in the Celtic year? Since the beginning of the century in Celtic terms would have been 01/11/01, it would be 1110 days. Or from the end of the previous century, 1111 days.

Isn't that utterly amazing?

Do you want more? Yet another 'coincidence' of much more recent times: the year 2011 is unique in this century because it contained the dates 1/1/11 and 11/1/11 and 1/11/11 and 11/11/11. The 111th day from the start of the year was Holy Thursday: the day when the Last Supper and the inauguration of the new covenant in Christ's blood is especially commemorated.[93]

The string-of-ones in 2011 was extensive. Take the last two digits of the year you were born and add the age you would have been on your birthday in 2011. If you were born this century, the answer will be 11. If you were born last century, the answer will be 111.

Are all these strings-of-ones just odd mathematical facts or do they form part of the fire-filled equations exhaled from God's breath? The concept of a string-of-ones is not recent. Its association with peace, tithing and covenant goes back four thousand years. Abraham offered a tithe to Melchizedek, king of Salem, when he came bearing bread and wine. Salem means *peace* and Melchizedek means *king of righteousness.* Bread and wine: signs of hospitality, symbols of an ancient salt and threshold covenant, tangible emblems which express the covenant partners' willingness to be truthful and faithful. Yes, indeed, those Four Daughters of God have been hanging out together for a very long time, along with a string-of-ones.

> *And Melchizedek, who was king of Salem and also a priest of the Most High God, brought bread and wine to Abram, blessed him, and said, 'May the Most High God, who made heaven and earth, bless Abram! May the Most High God, who gave you victory over your enemies, be praised!' And Abram gave Melchizedek a tenth of all the loot he had recovered.*
>
> Genesis 14:18–20 GNT

Tithing makes its second appearance in Scripture when Abraham's grandson Jacob has an experience of heaven meeting earth. Lying down to sleep one evening as he is fleeing home along with his brother's wrath, he dreamed of a ladder on which angels ascended and descended. On waking, he was struck by the realisation the Lord was in that place and so named it Bethel, *the house of God*.

> *He had a dream in which he saw a stairway resting on the earth, with its top reaching to heaven, and the angels of God were ascending and descending on it. There above it stood the Lord, and He said: 'I am the Lord, the God of your father Abraham and the God of Isaac... All peoples on earth will be blessed through you and your offspring. I am with you and will watch over you wherever you go...' When Jacob awoke from his sleep, he thought, 'Surely the Lord is in this place, and I was not aware of it.' He was afraid and said, 'How awesome is this place! This is none other than the house of God; this is the gate of heaven.' Early the next morning Jacob took the stone he had placed under his head and set it up as a pillar and poured oil on top of it. He called that place Bethel, though the city used to be called Luz. Then Jacob made a vow, saying, 'If God will be with me and will watch over me on this journey I am taking...then the Lord will be my God and this stone that I have set up as a pillar will be God's house, and of all that You give me I will give you a tenth.'*

Genesis 28:12–22 NIV

Like Ezekiel some 1500 years later, who was even more explicit that the place of Yahweh Shammah, *the Lord is there*, should encode a string-of-ones, he had a sense of how to re-affirm a covenant in a way our medieval ancestors thought massively important but that we have generally lost.

What's worse, the little we do understand, we do not see as an expression of faithfulness to God's covenant but as dispensable in our age of grace. Or as the belief of an unenlightened time when people still thought every slight action could have cosmic consequences.

We are casual—almost contemptuously so at times—about the eternal.

We have thrown out Justice and Truth and relied on Peace and Mercy to cover the holes in our armour and our inherited covenants.

6

Enthroned on High

IN THE BEGINNING *God created the heavens and the earth.*

On Christmas Eve 1968, as Apollo 8 orbited the moon, the three on-board astronauts controversially read from the book of Genesis. In Hebrew, the first verse they recited is seven words, one of which is never translated.

בְּרֵאשִׁית בָּרָא אֱלֹהִים אֵת הַשָּׁמַיִם וְאֵת הָאָרֶץ

bereshit bara Elokim et hashamaim v'et haarets [95]

The untranslated fourth word is simply two letters: 'alef' and 'tav'. They are the first and last letters of the Hebrew alphabet.

For many Christian scholars they are virtually insignificant, an 'untranslatable particle used to mark the definite object of the verb.'[96]

If you've already categorised this as Greek-influenced thinking, my personal opinion is that you'd be right. Because, for Jewish scholars, these two Hebrew letters are of immense significance when they are found together. The alef-tav combination is frequently found at the end of lines in ancient scrolls: the two letters are considered 'witnesses'[97] on behalf of the scribe that the text has been accurately copied. Alef-tav thus symbolises truth.

However, as the first and last letter of the Hebrew alphabet, the combination also symbolises the alphabet as a whole and thus, in addition, words.

Because alef-tav occurs in the phrase *bereshit bara Elokim et hashamaim v'et haarets* before the mention of the first created thing, the heavens, its positioning indicates that words are the very 'stuff' of creation. Words and letters therefore not only precede the creation of all things, they also describe the method of creation as well as form the vessel of creation.

They give shape to creation and are also witnesses to it.

Messianic believers, on the other hand, note that alef–tav by any other name is Alpha and Omega, the beginning and the end. They see it as a reference to Jesus, pre-eminent above creation and existing before the foundation of the world.[98]

The very first word in the Hebrew Bible is *bereshit.*

It's a poem, though generally it's simply translated 'In the beginning'. It has the following senses: *in, for, with, supreme, head, beginning, first.*

Both John and Paul attempted to open the bud and show the flower hidden within.

> In the **beginning** was the Word and the Word was **with** God and the Word was God. The same was in the **beginning with** God. All things were made by Him and without Him was not anything made that was made. In Him was life and the life was the light of men.

Of course, John—relational Hebrew thinker that he was— couldn't resist connecting *bereshit* to the other three words after it as well as to the Greek logos with its sense of word and of mathematics.

Paul, on the other hand, opens his epistle to the Colossians with another translation of the single word, *bereshit:*

> For by Him all things were created: things in Heaven and on earth, visible and invisible...all things were created by Him and **for** Him. He is **before** all things, and **in** Him all things hold

*together. And He is the **head** of the body, the church; He is the **beginning** and the **firstborn** from among the dead, so that in everything He might have the **supremacy**. For God was pleased to have all His fullness dwell in Him...*

Colossians 1:16–19 NIV

Here Paul is doing the same thing he did with nasa' in Ephesians 5 and 6: he's taking one Hebrew word and teasing out all its different senses as he translates the idea into another language.

And he's not just making verbal references: there are mathematical allusions here too. Greek thinking has a lot of fine points, despite its overall flaws. In the Greek way of addition, when numbers are summed up, the total goes at the top, not at the bottom.

We might say, 'Jesus is the bottom line,' but they would say, 'Jesus is the top line.'

He's the head who has everything under His feet. He's the answer to all of our needs in life—more than that, He is the Resurrection and the Life as well as the Way, the Truth and the Life. *No one comes to the Father, except through Him.*

And if you have problems with the exclusivity of the nature of that claim, ask yourself the question: which other religion actually has a loving Father as creator and covenant defender?

Is there any other religion where a deity says to each of us: *I love you enough to take your place, to exchange my life for your death, to lavish an inheritance on you just because, when I look at you, I see you as one with my darling Son, myself.*

The universe is made of words, not of atoms.

Muriel Rukeyser

From the very first verse of Scripture, the covenant nature of God is revealed. Not in the words, but in the mathematics.[99]

בְּתִישָׁאֶרֶ ב מִיק'לֵֶֶ אֶרְ **תֵא** םִיּמַשָׁהֶ תֵאֶן זְרֶאָה

These seven words—*bereshit bara Elokim et hashamaim v'et haarets*—are mathematically so rich and complex I'm just going to note some of what's there and encourage you to look further for yourself. These seven words contain 28 Hebrew letters.

Like the tetrakys of the Greeks, 28 forms a triangular number. In fact, 28 is the seventh triangular number. (The second verse has 14 words while verses 1 to 3 total 35 words, again multiples of 7.)

We should expect to find multiples of 111 in the first verse of Genesis. If, from the beginning God has been a covenant-keeping God, desiring oneness with His people and His creation, a string-of-ones should be encoded in the text.

Now when the text was first written down, letters and numbers were not separate. They were a fusion. So, we need to look into the gematria and calculate the numerical value of each word. Here are the results:

(A) bereshit = 913
(B) bara = 203
(C) Elokim = 86
(D) et = 401
(E) hashamayim = 395
(F) v'et = 407
(G) haarets = 296

The multiples of 111, the mathematical motif of covenant, are obvious:

A+C = 999

B+D+E = 999
C+E+F = 888

Of course, there are triangular numbers:

A+B+C+D+E+F+G = 2701 which has factors 73 and 37, whose sum is 110.

F+G = 703 which has factors 19 and 37.

In addition to these triangular numbers, there is another multiple of both 111 and 37 which is A+B+C+D+E = 1998 = 2 x 999 = 54 x 37

Note in all three cases, there is the common factor of 37. Why is it so important? Because it's one-third of 111, of course. That's where the string-of-ones is hidden.

And then, of course, the logos in its numerical form makes its appearance. Today we call the mathematical version of the logos 'the golden ratio' and it is approximately 0.618 to 1. This proportion appears everywhere in nature; it is so ubiquitous that I believe it to be the mark of the Creator—God's fingerprints, His signature—and that every created thing will show evidence of it in its design.[100] I also believe that, if we examine the mathematics, we can 'translate' it to find God's message to His creation—*I am Trinity, I am Love, I am Resurrection and Life.*

It goes without saying that David Howlett's discovery of the logos, the golden ratio, throughout Genesis 1 should be able to be extrapolated to Genesis 1:1. With a little calculation, it's very obvious:

○ B+G = 499
○ 499 divided by the logos is 808, the sum of D+F
○ 808 divided by the logos is 1307, the sum of B+D+F+G
○ 1307 divided by the logos is 2216, which is almost the sum of A+B+D+F+G at 2220.

In this verse are numerical symbols of covenant (111, 888, 999, 2220), of the Word and truth (499:808:1307:2220), of music and provision (808) and many other concepts not discussed here, including a preternaturally accurate value[101] of the irrational number, π.

The first line of the Hymn to the Logos in John 1:1 should be similar. In its 17 words and 52 letters, it actually goes so much further and is so dazzling I will simply direct you (with a warning that fairly serious mathematical ability is required) to the work of Richard McGough on the 'Logos Star' at the Bible Wheel archive.

However I also want to point out an aspect McGough does not—John 1:1 contains 777 in its gematria. I believe this is not only a reference to covenant (since it is a multiple of 111) but also to armour. At least Paul seemed to use it that way. In the Armour of God we have 77792 with its factors of 17 and 52 and indications of a string-of-sevens.

John 1:1 with 17 words and 52 letters and internal gematria of 777 reflects this. So Paul and John are on precisely the same page, whatever that page is. I believe the hidden layer, the *remez* or *derash*, for both of them is about threshold, beginning, covenant, troth.

Of all the places the armour of God is most needed is when crossing a spiritual threshold. We need to obey the laws of the threshold if we are ever to pass over it and enter the promise. Jesus made it clear that God's law could be distilled down to two commands, both of them about love.

Both of them essentially that of *nasa' keliy*—the uplifting, upbuilding armour-bearer.

My mum says I was born asking, 'Why?'

I'm sure she exaggerates. I'm sure it wasn't even my first word.

I don't even remember being relentless about *why* as a toddler, though she insists I was. I do remember my Grade Five teacher refusing to accept my book review unless I articulated why I liked *Anne of Green Gables*. I sat down, daunted at the prospect of having to fill an entire page with specific reasons and asking myself, 'So, Anne, why *do* you like it?' That's where, to the best of my memory, 'Why?' started for me.

My mother insists otherwise. She says, from the time I was an infant, I would never be fobbed off. I would never give up my inquisition until she gave me a reasonable explanation. Somehow this built into me the belief that, if I persisted, I'd find answers throughout life. Big ones.

It hasn't been until the last few years I realised most people never ever ask, 'Why?' Except at times of tragedy.

That's not the right time to start. If you're going to ask, 'Why, God?' and take up being a spiritual detective, it's wise to learn to read the clues He drops in your life.

Even those ones like a group of junior high girls reciting a putrid poem.

The past had a worldview so strange, so exotic, that most people of the twenty-first century would be more at home with a primitive jungle tribe than with their forebears of several centuries back. The perpetually-fed vision of the European Middle Ages as the Age of Faith in which knights did battle for the favour of beautiful ladies contains considerable romantic error.

The idea that most people were ignorant and illiterate is simply wrong. The notion that they thought the world was flat, not round, is mistaken.

As CS Lewis pointed out, more people thought the earth was flat in the nineteenth century than at any time during the Middle Ages.

As Louise Bishop has pointed out, women really did know how to read a millennium ago. The discovery of tens of thousands of fragments of well-used herbals and medical texts passed from mothers to their daughters indicate this. What 'uneducated' men and women didn't know how to read was Latin.[102]

A thousand years before, 'uneducated' men like Peter and John would have received at least three years of schooling in the Torah.

They would have had to have learned the Pentateuch—the first five books of Scripture—off by heart. They may even have made the cut as scholars and had an additional three years of education. In this case, they would have learned to recite the Prophets off by heart as well. However, at some stage, they failed to make it into tertiary education and were sent home to follow their fathers' trade.

Their second chance came when Jesus turned up and said, 'Come, follow Me,'—the traditional rabbi's invitation to finish their education with the interpretation of life experience.

'Uneducated', 'unschooled', 'illiterate'—all such terms are relative to their own age and culture. This is an important principle we tend to forget. So many Christians of today are proud of their ignorance, buoyed by the thought that Peter and John were 'ignorant fishermen'.

I use the adjective 'proud' carefully, meaning by it an attitude that openly vocalises: 'I'm just a simple Christian. I've never been any good at learning. This is too hard for me to understand.' This is not humility but pride. Inverted pride, it's true, but pride nonetheless. It's an excuse for shallow and lazy thinking, for anti-intellectualism and for not stretching God's gift of the mind to its full potential.

Love the Lord your God with all your heart and mind and soul and strength...

Jesus called this 'the greatest commandment in the Law.' Yet each of us is apt to ignore at least one of the four—heart, mind, soul or strength—just like we're apt to ignore at least one of the Four Daughters of God. I want you to think about the contents of this book. I don't want you to agree with everything I say. Some people will surely consider it eisegesis, an interpretation that expresses my own ideas and bias, rather than the meaning of the text. Sociologist Peter Berger once said: 'Whereas Judas betrayed Jesus with a kiss, today we betray him with a hermeneutic.'

So I want you to test what I've written. I want you to develop your gift of discernment, filter it through Scripture and, like the Bereans in the book of Acts, search through the Word of God to see how true it is.

Is Paul the misogynistic, chauvinistic hypocrite he's often portrayed as being? Or have we missed the point? And missed it again and again and again?

So many scholars delve deeply—sometimes even microscopically—into the meaning and background of various Greek words in order to illuminate the full robust sense of the text. Most of the time this will work well.

But occasionally, it's going to be a catastrophic failure. Paul was, by his own admission:

'circumcised when I was eight days old, having been born into a pure-blooded Jewish family that is a branch of the tribe of Benjamin. So I am a real Jew if there ever was one! What's more, I was a member of the Pharisees, who demand the strictest obedience to the Jewish law.'

Philippians 3:5 NLT

He was a Jew, writing in Greek. The unwritten assumption of much exegesis today is that Hebrew thought and Greek thought were virtually equivalent.

Paul threw all of his considerable rhetorical skills into ensuring his first century readers didn't get the wrong idea about hupotasso, *submit*. Faced with a monumental translation problem, he wrote paragraph after paragraph to guard against misunderstanding. Yet twenty centuries later, the man who eloquently wrote 'love is patient, love is kind...' has often been accused of giving licence to emotional and physical abuse.

Instead of focusing microscopically on the meaning of single Greek words, we *also* need to step back and view the entire passage in one light.

Sometimes we even have to do that for an entire book. As Richard Bauckham points out, John's gospel has the concentric structure of a Hebrew poem. John identifies himself as the author by placing the mention of 'disciple Jesus loved' at the end to match precisely the mention of John the Baptist at the beginning.

Now you're quite welcome to disagree with me but I believe that Paul and John, as well as all the other disciples and prophets whose works have been found to contain vast mathematical landscapes,[103] actually planned the numerical design beforehand. I don't believe the Holy Spirit downloaded the word–number fusion, dictating from heaven as they were writing and imposing an intricate structure as complex as DNA without their knowledge. The composition of the gospels and epistles was not 'automatic writing', an occult activity that bypasses the mind.

We are God's fellow-workers,[104] His beloved covenant partners, not His robots. I believe the Holy Spirit inspired His apostles and prophets to craft their writing so that the covenant-like oneness of words and numbers expressed a sublime universe of meaning. I don't think they always knew *all* they were writing,[105] but I believe God inspired them to plan out most of their artistry beforehand.

In an 'on-demand' age, the idea of such intensive, meticulous, careful and prayerful planning takes most of us aback. We can't imagine the patience of an artist who might take years to plan a single sentence. Or who might practise crafting a passage in several drafts—as Paul seems to have done in working his way up to the multi-layered artistry of the armour of God through his simpler practice runs of the armour of light and armour of righteousness.

Only some poets still polish like this.

We live in a superficial world, growing more shallow by the day. There's a tendency for many people to be cultural despisers of medieval knowledge, adopting the Enlightenment view that we have made huge advances in technology, so we must be superior. Few of us look closely enough at medieval writing to see how deeply they had immersed themselves in a Hebrew worldview. In fact, that idea is dismissed because we're all taught anti-Semitism was rife in the Middle Ages.

We're like 'Groupists' who, according to Herbert Henson, move at a stride from the Age of the Apostles to the present time, assuming that twenty centuries of Christian experience have nothing to teach us.[106]

The implications of George Santayana's famous quip, 'Those who cannot learn from history are doomed to repeat it,' elude us entirely.

So we let our own society dictate the filters we use to understand the Bible and we approach the Word of God in a mechanistic fashion. It's rare to see commentary that views any New Testament verse, let alone a passage, as the expression of a Hebrew thinker working in a second language.

It's no use thinking like scientific rationalists about the Bible. Yet that's basically the approach taken when we've analysed individual words in ever finer detail. This borders on Gnosticism: the elevation of knowledge to the position of saving faith.

Yet to disdain knowledge is also wrong.

Peter encourages us: '...*add to your faith goodness, and to goodness, knowledge...*'[107]

So, how do we get such a difficult balancing act just right?

Only through the oneness of covenant.

 נשׂא

Uplift is so important in God's economy it's imperative to get our sense of it right. Lucifer got it superlatively wrong: he is accused of puffing himself up and lifting himself against the Lord of Hosts. His desire was to set his throne above that of God. So:

I expelled you, O guardian cherub, from among the fiery stones. Your heart became proud on account of your beauty, and you corrupted your wisdom because of your splendour.

Ezekiel 28:16–17 NIV

Pharoah had the same lofty pride as Lucifer:

Pharaoh had a dream: he was standing by the Nile, when out of the river there came up seven cows, sleek and fat, and they grazed among the reeds.

Genesis 41:1–2 NIV

This was the beginning of the dream that troubled him enough to pluck a Hebrew slave out of prison to interpret it.

Jewish commentators note that, if translated literally, Pharoah in his dream would have been standing *over* the Nile, not *by* it.

The Nile River, in Egyptian understanding at that time, was a god. Pharoah had placed himself in his dream above the gods.

By contrast, a contemporary dream—that of Jacob who had a night vision of angels on a ladder—had a different feature:

*There **above** it stood the **Lord**.*

Genesis 28:13 NIV

Jacob at the bottom, the Lord at the top. Jacob was so awed by his dream, he promised to tithe. He was still a usurper at this stage, wrangling and manipulating for the best deal, but even he recognised the Lordship of heaven and earth.

Interestingly, Jewish commentators consider Pharoah's two dreams as being about the defilement that happens when a ruler usurps the place reserved for God. A defilement that ultimately resulted in a famine.

It's not only pride that can lead us down the path of usurpation. Curiously, pity can too. People who are natural burden-bearers and who have not had their talent redeemed can be so compassionate that they take on burdens they are not meant to carry. Here they enthrone themselves as redeemer. Buried so deep in their hearts they are not even aware of it is a doubt so insatiable it will eventually—except for God's mercy—consume them. And that hidden doubt can be articulated something like this: *God cannot fix this situation, so I have to.*

This is pride of the most subtle kind: the belief that I could do a better job of running my small corner of the universe than God can.

A toxic mix of doubt and pride, hidden under the desire to help others, is as defiling as the curse Pharoah inflicted on Egypt. No wonder he was prepared to give Joseph and Joseph's merciful God a chance to avert the consequences of the coming famine.

As a paraclete, as an armour-bearer, we have to keep our armour in trim. A toxic vow or a hidden prideful belief in us means our shield of faith has a mighty gaping hole in it. It's useless against the enemy darts fired at us.

And of course the more we are hit by enemy darts, the more our doubts that God can take care of the situation are reinforced. And the more likely our resolve is to work harder at ensuring our loved ones are protected. We will do it, if God cannot.

This is not armour-bearing.

We're called to submit to God, not usurp. We're called to lift up God, not hold Him under. We're called to carry one another's burdens, not our own and someone else's. We're called to surrender our hearts to God, not reserve a small hidden corner of it, through fear He might trample on it rather than cherish it.

We're called to be one with Him, not half with Him.

We're called to be princes with God. One word for prince is *nasi*, which is—naturally—derived from *nasa'*.

Perhaps it was even in Paul's thoughts when he wrote, 'Submit to the governing authorities.' Two forms of nasa' together make perfect sense: *lift up the princes*. The implication: they will lift you so together you build a nation rising to greatness and drawing others to the holy uplifted Name of God.

As any physicist will tell you: there is no such thing as a perpetual motion principle.

Yet God has structured the universe so that one seed yields a hundred—one act of lovingkindness will yield enough to upbuild a community.

A true prince is not arrogant, not boastful, not rude, not self-seeking, not easily angered, keeps no record of wrongs.

He (or she) simply lifts up and is lifted up and lifts up and...

...one Lord, one faith, one baptism, one God and Father of all, who is over all and through all and in all.

Ephesians 4:5–6 NIV

7

Morning has Broken

MANY YEARS AGO I REMEMBER reading a novel in which one of the characters spent his days searching through dusty scrolls for a copy of an ancient prophecy. Although the character was frustrated by the task, I personally thought I would like nothing better. It wasn't the finding of a prophecy that attracted me, it was the treasure trove of knowledge that would be unearthed along the way.

'...*add to your faith goodness, and to goodness, knowledge...*' [107]

One of the reasons I love delving into medieval poetry is because it exposes my own cultural biases. One of the reasons I love comparing the mathematics there to that of the Greek New Testament is because it forces me to think about the Scripture in ways that have not been conditioned by my upbringing or the latest methodology in exegesis.

It's rare for me these days to be shocked by the discovery of a hidden prejudice, but it still happens.

Just a few days ago I was reading a book I've been trying to get a copy of for some time: Kenneth Bailey's *Poet and Peasant*.

Bailey looks at the parables of Luke in this volume in an exceedingly interesting way. Having lived for some years in the Middle East, he is familiar with the languages there and with the New Testament in several different tongues of the region, including Syriac and Arabic. From this he suggests reconstructions of the original Aramaic for several of Jesus' parables.

What emerges is stunning.

It's poetry—verse that's exquisite, intricate, technically dazzling, unquestionably memorable, irresistibly playful.

I have no problem with that: God, as I have repeatedly maintained in *God's Poetry: The Identity and Destiny Encoded in Your Name*, is a master versifier.

What shocked me was Bailey's comment about one brilliant poem which he said was: *'...the work of a skilled... poet in the first century. There remains no reason to doubt that the author was Jesus of Nazareth.'*

That remark was, I'm sure, intended to counter any thought that the poetic parable was the work of a literary genius in the Christian community. Yet it exposed an attitude in me I wasn't aware of: I had thought I considered Jesus to be extremely intelligent, not an uneducated rustic preacher. But the idea that he was a literary master was so startling I realised there were quite a few vestiges left in me of the anti-intellectualism rampant in many parts of Christianity today.

'Poetry,' said Robert Frost, *'is what gets lost in translation.'*

That is self-evident.

I've read many different translations of my favourite medieval poem, *Sir Gawain and the Green Knight*. Some of them are prose renditions which leave no sense of either the verse or the mathematical structure. Some are stiff and starchy and others are rollicking romps: the best of them are always translated not by academics, but by poets.

Jesus of Nazareth: an incomparable poet.

Thinking of Jesus as a virtuoso of words is going to take some getting used to. I've too long lived in a culture where the followers of Jesus, as well as His detractors, see the parables as simple story-telling. And by 'simple', I suddenly realise, we've probably meant 'simplistic'.

In Arabic, the name for the followers of Jesus is an unusual one. Their word for Christians is 'nasara'—it's a name they connect back to 'Nazareth' although they give it the meaning *helpers, supporters* or *assisters.*

The commentary on nasara shows it is clearly related to nasa', *lift off.* Yet, in Strong's, the most common Bible lexicon, the name Nazareth is said to mean *the guarded one*, its derivation being 'of unknown origin'. Cornwall & Smith's *The Exhaustive Dictionary of Bible Names* suggests *preserved* or *branch.*

On the one hand we have the suggestion of *helpers* from *lift off* and, on the other, *guarded, preserved* or *branch.*

Surely the idea that combines all of these senses so that they are part of each other as a branch is part of a vine is that of a covenant defender, an armour-bearer. The one who submits by lifting up.

Ironically, the Arabic name for Christians, *nasara*, counterpoints the word *Islam.* Both mean *submission.*

Though, of course, they have different senses.

So does Nazareth mean *the place of an armour-bearer, the town of the covenant defender?* Surely nothing could be more appropriate as the name of a town where Jesus would grow up.

I have to suspect there was a huge beaming smile on Luke's face when he finished writing the story of Jesus in the Temple at age twelve. After stunning the doctors of the Law with His wisdom and knowledge, Jesus floored Mary and Joseph with a casual reminder of who He really is. But then, after this reunion with His mother and foster-father, '...He went down to Nazareth and was submissive to them.'[108]

If Nazareth and nasa' are related, this is just the sort of play on words Luke would have known that Jesus Himself loved.

Even if it, too, has been lost in translation.

Jesus, like the prophets before Him, seems to have taken great delight in adding a fun element to His words.

Children, obey your parents in the Lord for this is right.

Ephesians 6:1 NIV

In between the discussion that starts, '*Wives, submit to your husbands*' and the commentary of the Armour of God, Paul adds a few words on obedience to children and slaves.

Let's face it: this too is about nasa'—*submission* in the sense of *lifting up*.

If there is a single melody line connecting all the writing in the New Testament, from the biographical Gospels to the pastoral epistles, surely it is the theme of nasa' in all its symphonic grace. Like a lark ascending, it fills the air with the sweet music of lifting off, lifting up, forgiveness, removal of sin, burden–bearing, helping, supporting, covenant, submission, obedience, oneness.

Armour-bearing.

So: '*...add to your faith goodness, and to goodness, knowledge... self–control... perseverance... godliness... kindness... love.*'

One...

From babyhood, we're taught to see the world through western rationalist eyes. Even a simple thing like a first counting book teaches a particular mindset. 'One' is solitary, 'two' is a duplicated clone of one, 'three' is presented as a set of identical triplets.

However, three matching cats sitting on three matching mats confuses 'triple' with 'three'. The nature of threeness transcends that of tripleness. The three bears with their three chairs encountered by Goldilocks are more true to the concept of 'three' than most books designed specifically to teach children to count.

In this day and age it's difficult to think of numbers as religious in nature. It's hard to imagine the pitched battles over whether numbers were gods. In fact, it's almost impossible to understand why there was violent opposition to the concept of 'zero' in the Middle Ages.

Mathematics today is seen as so unassailably neutral.

Yet zero, introduced by way of Arab scholarship from the Hindu system, originated in the idea of nirvana. The psychological shift this produced in western culture was nothing short of stupendous. Once you can conceive of a number as 'nothing' and apply it in the trade of goods, it's a short step to conceiving of human beings as nothing. And then as less than nothing.

Life might have been cheap in the Middle Ages but there was never any question it had value.

There is a colossal chasm between nothingness and oneness.

On the far side of the bridge crossing that chasm is not simply 'one' but all of creation in one.

It was for this reason that the medieval worldview with its interconnected oneness was torn asunder as the decimal system replaced Roman numerals. Unified 'oneness' gave way to the singularity of 'one'.

The void opened up as connection was lost. And the void has remained.

The Middle Ages is seen as the Age of Faith. Yet it was a battleground with resurgent neo-Platonism coupled with neo-Pythagoreanism. In other words, a new breed of Christianity's ancient enemy, Gnosticism.

On balance, despite several major defeats, Christianity held the line for centuries. But then a second front opened up: a new number system with a new religious base—the Hindu-Arabic system.

The Hebrew mindset which, despite the odds, had actually prevailed in the Christian world began to collapse.

To the Jewish mind, a person is not a solitary 'one' but rather a unity of body, mind and soul/breath expressed in the Hebrew word נפש, *nephesh.* This unity reaches out to a wider community.

Jeff Benner points out the similarity with a tree: it is a unity of roots, trunk, branches and leaves which are in turn in unity with the wider landscape. The first use of אחד, 'ehad' meaning *one,* in Scripture demonstrates this idea of unity. It is found in Genesis 1:5

where evening and morning combine to form 'one' day.[109]

The night is nearly over; the day is almost here. So let us put aside the deeds of darkness and put on the armour of light.

Romans 13:12 NIV

Here is the culmination of Paul's dance with nasa' in his letter to the Romans. He starts with submit to the governing authorities, moves on to law which is summed up in the command to love and then goes on to say: *the night is nearly over, the day is almost here.*

He's describing the time of morning twilight, that indigo glow just before the dawn.

The special word for this in Hebrew is nesheph, from nashaph, *to blow.*

All through this sequence in Paul's letter to the Romans is the thought: nasa', *lift up.* If you look closely, you'll realise it was never far from his mind.

The armour of light, just like the armour of God, is designed for a special task: to lift us up so we can lift up others.

Now, you may also have noticed that nashaph, *to blow*, bears some similarity to naphash, *breath, to refresh.*

This word naphash is said to be the more common variant of nashaph[110] and both are cognates for the words we have already seen are inextricably entwined: breath, soul and name.

A woman came to talk to me about a unique problem. Her mother had rejected her so completely at birth that she had refused to be involved in choosing her name. Her father and grandmother had taken her off to be christened regardless. For a start, this woman wasn't sure she'd been given God's name for her. And, she wanted to know, if covenants exist over names and draw us into our destiny (or hinder us from crossing over the threshold into it), how would she have been affected by growing up with a mother who had rejected the most basic aspect of her identity?

I asked her if she had any problem with breathing. I was

thinking about the possibility of asthma, sinus problems, chronic respiratory issues. I certainly wasn't expecting what she said next. 'I'm much better than I used to be,' she reported, 'but the sound of other people's breathing drives me crazy.'

I held my breath for several seconds before realising what an absurd reaction it was. I turned to her husband and said, 'That must be hell to live with.'

'Tell me about it,' he said.

The visible expression of her complicity with the rejection of her name and thus her soul was in her exasperation with the sound others made when they breathed.

As it turned out, when we progressed into prayer ministry, the defilement that had begun with her mother had spread out. The only person she would ever have been comfortable with as a husband was one who had rejected his own name. So when, quite by accident (the sort of one the Holy Spirit orchestrates), it came out her husband's name wasn't really John, it was really a surprise. Not even his children knew his original given name.

When you are dealing with name covenants, you're doing soul surgery. That can be very traumatic. Usually I prescribe a gentle medication: simply ask Jesus of Nazareth to step into your name and make it a gate of praise.

It's not something that bears fruit overnight. It's slow but it's effective.

There are, however, cases like those of John where radical surgery is required.

There's a reason for this. Please pardon me if I explain it in mathematical terms.

Suppose your name is Shem. Your name, like any other name, encodes the purpose and meaning of your life and what you stand for as a part of God's body. It should be composed of equal parts of identity and destiny. For the sake of argument, let identity be given the value 10 and destiny also be 10. Together they are multiplied to make 100%.

The value of your name stays constant at 100% of who you are meant to be. However, life presents you with choices, sometimes invidious ones. On the threshold of your destiny, as the gates open wide to usher you into your calling, you will invariably be asked to make a choice and offer a sacrifice. The price of crossing the threshold will always, by the nature of the spiritual dynamic, be one you are reluctant to pay. You will be faced with an ethical dilemma. You'll be asked to choose between the integrity of your character and the promise of the future—that is, your identity will be pitted against your destiny.

I give some real–life examples of this situation in *God's Poetry*.

Suppose you choose identity over destiny: then the identity component of your name might go up to 20 and the destiny down to 5. It's like this:

Identity: 20   **Destiny**: 5   **Name**: 20x5 = 100

You encounter another opportunity to come into your destiny. The door seems open. But then the 'catch' becomes apparent. Again you choose identity over destiny.

Identity: 50   **Destiny**: 2   **Name**: 50x2 = 100

It happens again.

Identity: 100   **Destiny**: 1   **Name**: 100x1 =100

And again.

Identity: 10000   **Destiny**: 0.01 **Name**: 10000 x 0.01 = 100

Your destiny is shunted aside so far at this point, you've probably given up. Every time the door opens, it either slams in your face or leads into a meaningless labyrinth: you go in, you come back out again and you're not sure what happened. The door might have been open but the breakthrough just wasn't there. It was like wandering around in the wilderness, marking time.

Now the fact is, your name is still your name. Value 100%.

You want your destiny back, and you'd prefer it to be at least to the 10 you were given in the first place. But you certainly don't want to lose all the character formation that has occurred along the way.

No way do you want that dark night of the soul you experienced to count for nothing. You actually don't want the value of your identity to slide from 10000 or a million back down to 10.

That's why the value of your name needs to change. Not your identity but your *name*. The one constant value in this equation has to undergo an impossible transformation. It needs to be worth more than 100%! The only way it can do that is if you invite Jesus to step over the threshold into it. Because He has that precious oneness with the infinite God, He is able to change its value. Just as God stepped into Abram's name and changed it to Abraham, so your destiny will change when Jesus steps into yours.

There is a sense in which we have to make our names into theophorics: that is, names that carry the name of God. But we also need to be very careful not to assume that the theophoric names of old—like Daniel, *God is a judge*, or Michael, *who is like God*—have not been corrupted over the centuries by different cultural accretions.

These issues are discussed at length in *God's Poetry*.

In addition there may be bindings and seals and curses coming down many generations that are like strangleholds over names. In fact, it's almost certain some of these issues will be present. In influencing your name, they affect your soul as well as your destiny. However, when Jesus, the paraclete, comes to dwell within 'the house' of your name, He'll begin to deal with those issues.

Asking Jesus to step into your name, surrendering it to Him so He can purify it, is simply going right back to a beginning: as God breathed life into your soul by giving you a part of His name, so now you are returning that part of His name to Him to get it sorted. Where He's been kicked out, you're asking Him back. You are inviting Him to allow His Spirit to blow wherever He wills. There are undoubtedly some dark corners that need a good brisk breeze into them.

The Paraclete will ask you to work with Him from time to time in this process. Confession, forgiveness, repentance and renunciation will be part of it.

As each hole in the armour of light closes up, you'll be lifted up and be better able to lift others up. Whether the armour is meant for defence or for attack, one thing is sure: it doesn't weigh you down. Its special property is to lift us up so we can in turn lift others up and, in so doing, lift up the name of God.

As your broken heart heals and your soul unites to 'fear' God's name, your name will come to reference and reverence His. You'll become an armour-bearer. A paraclete. A companion for battle.

Your oneness with Him as you come into this calling gives you authority to call on His name. As mentioned previously, Jesus told His disciples to ask the Father in His name only as He instituted the new covenant in His blood. He specifically said:

'Up to this time you have not asked a [single] thing in My Name [as presenting all that I AM] but now ask and keep on asking and you will receive...'

John 16:24 AMP

Here is the institution of name exchange that is part of the sevenfold covenant ceremony.

The deeper significance of Jesus' words at this time is that He invests each of His disciples with the authority of a *shaliach*. This word comes from shalach, *sent*, and means a messenger sent in another's name, an emissary with delegated authority. He's an envoy who carries more than a message, he also carries power. He represents his master in every way—there is a sense in which he *actually is* the master.

This is why, when Jacob wrestles with an angelic messenger, he's wrestling with God. It's why Joshua's encounter with the Commander of the Armies of the Lord is a meeting with God Himself. The *shaliach* should be able to expect the honour and respect due to his master. If a *shaliach* steps outside the bounds of his authority then his abuse of power will bring trouble on his own head.

Because his power is absolute: as an ambassador plenipotentiary, he has the right to commit an entire nation to war. Or proclaim peace.

Jesus, the armour-bearer, the paraclete, the shaliach, appointed each of His followers to the same role through our covenantal oneness with Him. He entrusted us with extraordinary power. Thus our prayers in Jesus' name need to be totally aligned with His will. Because the power He gives us is conditional: our prayers will not be answered if they are outside His will.

When we attempt to control others through prayer, manipulate or direct them along a particular path, we're outside His will. He is not a thief: He will never rob anyone of their free will. When we pray like this, we mix faith and magic. We're casting spells and sometimes even flinging curses in an attempt to make the world conform to what we think it should be.

There's another word for *ambassador* in Hebrew besides *shaliach*. It's *tsiyr* which also means *the hinge of a door*.

It took me a while to wrap my thinking around that concept: an ambassador is a hinge, a living join between two nations, two peoples, two societies, two cultures.

Jesus, the Son sent from the Father, is not only a *shaliach* but the hinge[111] between heaven and earth, light and dark, spirit and flesh.

The apostles, *the sent ones*, were like God's angel messengers, who were also *sent ones*. This is our work in the world: to take on the role of a shaliach. The word 'labour' in English is related to *pain*, but in Hebrew it's related to *angel*.

True work is therefore being an angel. A messenger. A sent one. An ambassador. A hinge in your nation or neighbourhood between God and other people.

Every shaliach needs a paraclete, an armour-bearer. Because, by himself, he may be able to put a thousand enemies to flight, but with a wingman covering his back, they can—so Deuteronomy 32:30 says—send ten thousand fleeing away.

This mathematics suggests that it would take between seven and eight people to change the entire world. United with one vision, one with each other and with God, anointed as ambassadors, they could turn the whole world upside down. As Philippians 2:2 NLT says: '[agree] wholeheartedly with each other, loving one another, and working together with one mind and purpose.'

You're called to be part of that company.

One of the princes of God—a *nasi*.

So put on the armour of God. And remember to lift your face for His kiss.

Endnotes

1 Marina Warner, *Joan of Arc—The Image of Female Heroism*, University of California Press

2 Mark 5:41

3 John 1:42

4 Mark 15:34

5 Bishop KC Pillai in his work, *Light Through an Eastern Window*, suggests this may be better translated: *'My God, my God, for this I was born! This is my destiny!'*

6 Graham Cooke, *God's Keeping Power: Learning to put your trust in God as your "keeper"*, Brilliant Book House 2004

7 Joseph Pearce, *Tolkien: Man and Myth*, Harper Collins 1999

8 *But Ruth said, 'Do not press me to leave you or to turn back from following you! Where you go, I will go; where you lodge, I will lodge; your people shall be my people, and your God my God. Where you die, I will die—there will I be buried. May the Lord do thus and so to me, and more as well, if even death parts me from you!'* (Ruth 1:16–17 NRS) Perhaps it is no surprise, given this statement of Ruth's, that her name means *friend.*

9 See Fred Handschumacher, *The Rock of Offence*, http://www.rockofoffence. com/sec1.pdf In total agreement with Handschumacher, I reiterate his emphatic statement that this book in no way advocates that anyone should go out and engage in a blood covenant rite today. Rather its purpose is to alert us to the possible reaping in our own lives of what our ancestors may have sown in regard to covenants.

10 Ephesians 5:23 KJV

11 1 Corinthians 11:3–15

12 Note that Paul says men should not have their heads covered while praying. Exactly the opposite prevails when Jewish men pray in public today. Either customs have changed for the Jewish people in the last 2000 years or Paul had reached another conclusion about head covering from his study of Scripture and rabbinical literature.

13 Song of Songs 2:4 NAS For an utterly beautiful version which is both poetic and retains the Hebrew sense throughout, there is no finer translation at present than Brian Simmons' *The Most Amazing Song of All*, which is part of *The Passion Translation.*

14 In *Healing the Masculine Soul*, Gordon Dalbey refers to John Sandford's teaching (audiotape *A Closer Look 10*) and says that, when Jesus refers to the Holy Spirit as the Helper, he uses a Greek word, *paraclete*, that was an ancient warrior's

term. 'Greek soldiers went into battle in pairs,' says Dalbey, 'so when the enemy attacked, they could draw together back-to-back, covering each other's blind side. One's battle partner was the paraclete.' Our Lord does not send us to fight the good fight alone. The Holy Spirit is our battle partner who covers our blind side and fights for our well-being.

15 The English word translated 'advocate' comes from the Greek *parakletos*. 'Para–' is a prefix meaning *alongside*. 'Kletos' means *to be called, appointed* or *invited*. In a law court, it referred to a defence counsel who came alongside you, while in military terms it meant the 'wingman' who would turn to fight back to back with you in the fiercest conflict.

16 Deuteronomy 4:48— *From Aroer, which is by the bank of the river Arnon, even unto mount Sion, which is Hermon*

17 Isaiah 1:18

18 Psalm 22:1; 6

19 Although many lexicons give Zion as meaning *dry* or *parched*, Wikipedia suggests the following: The etymology of the word *Zion* (*ṣiyôn*) is uncertain. Mentioned in the Bible in the Book of Samuel (2 Samuel 5:7) as the name of the Jebusite fortress conquered by King David, its origin likely predates the Israelites. If Semitic, it may be derived from the Hebrew root *ṣiyyôn* ('castle') or the Hebrew *ṣiyya* ('dry land', Jeremiah 51:43) or the Arabic *šanā* ('protect' or 'citadel'). It might also be related to the Arabic root *ṣahî* ('ascend to the top') or *ṣuhhay* ('tower' or 'the top of the mountain'). A non-Semitic relationship to the Hurrian word *šeya* ('river' or 'brook') has also been suggested.

20 Deuteronomy 3:8-9 says: *So at that time we took from these two kings of the Amorites the territory east of the Jordan, from the Arnon Gorge as far as Mount Hermon. (Hermon is called Sirion by the Sidonians; the Amorites call it Senir.)*

Senir or Shenir means *snow mountain*, deriving from tsinnah, meaning *something piercing, hook, barb, coldness (of snow), shield* or *buckler*.

Hermon is often said to mean *sanctuary*.

21 Philippians 2:1-2 NRS

22 Matthew 6:26 CEV

23 The collective noun for a group of geese in flight is *wedge* or *skein*. The collective noun for a group of geese on the ground is *gaggle*.

24 Genesis 22:13

25 Ezekiel 40:14

26 Isaiah 1:29

27 Exodus 15:15

God's Panoply

28   http://www.torah.org/features/par-kids/names.html

29   I apologise in advance to those people who have studied the Hebrew language and to whom this concept will be confrontational but I see two overlapping words at the beginning of nashamah—nasha (the same as nasa, *lift up*) and sham (the same as shem, *the name*). There may also be a third word here: shammah, *present, here*. This last reflects the name of the City of God in Ezekiel 49: Yahweh Shammah, *the Lord is here*.

My observations of how people use their own names indicate that sounds, even overlapping sounds, even elisions where some sounds disappear should not be discounted. Even rhymes sometimes. This is why I called the first book in this series about names and covenants *God's Poetry*—because not only does Ephesians 2:10 say explicitly we are God's poetry (though usually translated *workmanship*) but because that is what I observe. I note also that the prophets used the concept of rhyme (both head–rhyme and tail–rhyme, though more of the former), assonance and other poetic sound devices extensively in prophecy where they connected the destiny of a place to the meaning of a word that *sounded* like the name of the location. Thus I feel often that even the modern study of Biblical Hebrew has taken on a Greek cast and I would argue that both **sounds** and letters are significant in understanding words.

30   adam

31   adamah

32   John 16:24

33   If you are keen to do this but have no idea how to begin, may I suggest my own book, the first in this series — *God's Poetry: The Identity and Destiny Encoded in Your Name*.

34   http://bit.ly/PBDkNw

35   Though I'm mixing my fantasy authors fairly seriously here. *Discovering truth in what you write* is a sentiment from George MacDonald.

36   Some years ago, I read an interesting newspaper comment which said that judicial systems based on the Westminster model are not actually designed to bring about the most just outcome; however, the French system along with some other European ones are structured along these lines. I am unsure if this is actually true, but I always considered it a remarkable statement on the inherent injustice of many sentences today. In Australia, you'll spend longer in jail for accepting a political bribe than for murder.

37   A term of Harvard law professor Mary Ann Glendon.

38   Simon Wiesenthal, *The Sunflower*; Foreword by Os Guinness, Trinity Forum Reading Spring 2000

39   *Above all else, guard your heart, for it is the wellspring of life.* Proverbs 4:23 NIV

The heart is deceitful above all things and beyond cure. Who can understand it?
Jeremiah 17:9 NIV

40   Simon Wiesenthal, *The Sunflower*; Foreword by Os Guinness, Trinity Forum
      Reading Spring 2000

41   Armour of light is in Romans 13:12, armour of God in Ephesians 6 and
      individual pieces in 1 Thessalonians 5:8

42   Known as *halisah* in Hebrew.

43   LITV (Green's Literal Translation Version)

44   Jeff A Benner, *The Ancient Hebrew Language and Alphabet: Understanding the
      Ancient Hebrew Language of the Bible Based on the Ancient Hebrew Culture and
      Thought*, 2004

45   Little wonder that Peter's letters are peppered with references to the church as
      living stones.

46   Loricas are thought to be inspired by the admonition of Paul in Ephesians 6:14
      to put on the breastplate of righteousness. Generally, loricas were very long
      prayers or songs. To listen to a very beautiful (and long) lorica by St Brendan
      of Clonfert (famous for his voyage to what was almost certainly America some
      eight or nine centuries before Columbus), go to:

      http://archive.org/details/LoricaBrendan

      The following text is the beginning of a lorica by St Gildas. In the original
      language, it is written in a metre of eleven syllables called *bracicatalecticon*.
      This point is noted in the light of the significance of 11 (and also 22) later
      in this book. The remainder of the lorica by Gildas requests, in somewhat
      exhaustive detail, a multitude of specific body parts to be shielded and covered
      by God.

      Help unity of trinity,
      have pity trinity of unity;
      Help me, I pray, thus placed
      as in the peril of a great sea,
      So that the plague of this year
      draw me not with it, nor the vanity of the world.
      And this very petition I make unto the high
      powers of the heavenly warfare,
      that they leave me not to be harried by enemies,
      but defend me with their strong armour;
      that, before me in the battle, go
      those armies of the heavenly warfare,
      Cherubim and Seraphim with their thousands,
      Gabriel and Michael with like ones.
      May thrones, powers, archangels,

principalities, dominions, angels,
defend me with their thick array,
and be strong to overthrow my enemies.
Then also the other arbiters of the strife—
patriarchs four, prophets four,
Apostles, watchmen of the ship of Christ,
And the athlete martyrs all—I ask,
And adjure also all virgins,
faithful widows, and confessors,
that safety compass me by them,
and every evil perish from me.
May Christ make with me a strong covenant,
He whose terror scares away the foul throngs.

47   This is the covenant with death, mentioned in Isaiah 28:16. It is not, as it sounds, a death wish. Just the opposite. It begins with a total loss of faith in God and a belief that nothing is as powerful as Death. A covenant with death is an agreement with a personified spirit of Death to protect a family from itself. This perversion of a covenant offers Death the destiny of a family in exchange for survival. For more detail on symptoms and issues, see *God's Poetry: The Identity and Destiny Encoded in Your Name.*

48   In *God's Poetry: The Identity and Destiny Encoded in Your Name*, I contend that it means *my right hand*, not *usurper*. I believe it is derived from Jamin (as in Benjamin), not from Jacob.

49   The five-pointed star was symbolic of truth and Christ at the time, a natural association since it is an iconic form containing the golden ratio which happens to have been called the *logos* in Greek.

50   In *God's Poetry: The Identity and Destiny Encoded in Your Name*, I look at the relationship between the name Lewis preferred—'Jack'—the recurring image that came to his mind's eye for several decades and the book inspired by the image: *The Lion, The Witch and the Wardrobe.*

51   1 Thessalonians 5:11 NIV

52   Galatians 6:9

53   2 Thessalonians 3:13 NKJV

54   John Loren & Paula Sandford, *Letting Go of Your Past*, Charisma House 2008

55   As an editor, I find it easier to work with mediocre stories, rather than good ones: the chances I will get caught up in the story and overlook errors are less. There are writing techniques to help achieve this very aspect of reader-character oneness. A reader won't notice these in a fine story but will find them irritating in a mediocre one.

56   Mark D. Roberts in the Daily Reflection from *www.TheHighCalling.org*

commented that this *'is one of the most complex sentences in all of Scripture. This is not only because of its length (which, in the age of Twitter seems mammoth—there are more words here than Twitter allows in characters!) It is also because the nature of Greek allows for considerable variability in the connections made between phrases. For example, the phrase 'in love' in verse 4 can go with what proceeds 'he chose us in love' or what follows 'he predestined us in love.' The finest scholars have not come to a consensus on which option is the best one.'*

Here we go with the one sentence translated into English, which in fact needs more words and weighs in at a stupendous 281: *Praise be to the God and Father of our Lord Jesus Christ, who has blessed us in the heavenly realms with every spiritual blessing in Christ, for he chose us in him before the creation of the world to be holy and blameless in his sight and in love he predestined us to be adopted as his sons through Jesus Christ, in accordance with his pleasure and will—to the praise of his glorious grace, which he has freely given us in the One he loves, so that, in him we have redemption through his blood, the forgiveness of sins, in accordance with the riches of God's grace that he lavished on us with all wisdom and understanding; and he made known to us the mystery of his will according to his good pleasure, which he purposed in Christ, to be put into effect when the times will have reached their fulfilment—to bring all things in heaven and on earth together under one head, even Christ, in whom we were also chosen, having been predestined according to the plan of him who works out everything in conformity with the purpose of his will, in order that we, who were the first to hope in Christ, might be for the praise of his glory—and you also were included in Christ when you heard the word of truth, the gospel of your salvation, for, having believed, you were marked in him with a seal, the promised Holy Spirit, who is a deposit guaranteeing our inheritance until the redemption of those who are God's possession—to the praise of his glory.*

57   In fact, he was the first to translate into Latin from Hebrew, rather than from the revered Greek Septuagint. David Howlett in *British Books in Biblical Style* creates a number of examples to demonstrate the kind of mathematical designs copied by the numerical literary artists of the Dark Ages and early medieval times. These include the Hebrew text of Genesis 1, the Vulgate translation of Genesis 1 and the Septuaguint translation of Genesis 1. It is clear from Howlett's analysis that Jerome made a valiant attempt to reproduce the mathematical design as well, while the translators of the Greek Septuaguint did not.

58   If there is a number symbolising 'completeness' (and I'm not sure there is), it's probably 22.

59   The original obviously did not have the verse numbering in it, since the divisions into chapter and verse did not come about until the era of the printing press. For the quote, see for example *The Dignity of Difference*, Jonathan Sacks 2003

60   The original version of this hymn was written by Welsh poet William Rees,

better known in Wales by his bardic name Gwilym Hiraethog. He was a farmer's son from North Wales, born in 1802 at a farm called Chwibren Isaf near Llansannan in Denbighshire. His father's family originally came from Wenvoe in South Wales, while his mother's family was descended from one of the very ancient royal families of Gwynedd in North Wales, whose genealogy can be traced back as far as the third century.

61   *Therefore put on the full armour of God, so that when the day of evil comes, you may be able to stand your ground...with the belt of truth buckled around your waist, with the breastplate of righteousness in place, and with your feet fitted with the readiness that comes from the gospel of peace. In addition to all this, take up the shield of faith, with which you can extinguish all the flaming arrows of the evil one. Take the helmet of salvation and the sword of the Spirit, which is the word of God. And pray in the Spirit on all occasions with all kinds of prayers and requests. With this in mind, be alert and always keep on praying for all the saints.* Ephesians 6:12–18 NIV

Everyone must submit himself to the governing authorities, for there is no authority except that which God has established... Let no debt remain outstanding, except the continuing debt to love one another, for he who loves his fellowman has fulfilled the law. The commandments...are summed up in this one rule: 'Love your neighbour as yourself.' Love does no harm to its neighbour. Therefore love is the fulfilment of the law. And do this, understanding the present time. The hour has come for you to wake from your slumber, because our salvation is nearer now than when we first believed. The night is nearly over; the day is almost here. So let us put aside the deeds of darkness and put on the armour of light. Romans 13:1–12 NIV

But since we are of the day, let us be sober, having put on the breastplate of faith and love, and as a helmet, the hope of salvation. 1 Thessalonians 5:8 NAS

In pureness, in knowledge, in patience, in kindness, in the Ruach HaKodesh, in sincere love, in the word of truth, in the power of God; by the armour of righteousness on the right hand and on the left. 2 Corinthians 6:6–7 HNV

62   See, for instance, Kerry M. Olitzky, Ronald H. Isaacs, *I Believe: The Thirteen Principles of Faith : A Confirmation Textbook*, KTAV Publishing 2003. As I wrote this section, the daily devotional from Rabbi Eckstein, *The Angel's Dispute*, was on just this topic. The midrashic teaching has been a little updated in the last thousand years: when the Messiah comes, the fight between the angels will turn to a kiss.

63   The major scholarly study on the Four Daughters of God is over a century old: Hope Traver, *The Four Daughters of God, A Study of the Versions of this Allegory with Especial Reference to those in Latin, French and English*, The John C Winston Co, 1907. Traver makes the very significant note (though it's only in a footnote) this Midrashic story can only have arisen after Aramaic supplanted Hebrew, since it interprets Psalm 85 on the basis there are two words of double meaning: 'meet' means 'fight' and 'kiss' is taken as 'arm one's self'.

64   Note the repetition of the word for *stand*. Coming from the word for pillars or

doorposts, it can be symbolic of the two sides of a doorway.

65   What you use to step over a threshold

66   The word used means *underbinding*. Bindings on a doorway may refer to the words spoken (or written) to secure the doorway. Similar to those found in a mezuzah.

67   The word used here is the same word as that used for the Day of Preparation.

68   The same word is used for a door.

69   The word used for arrows or darts comes from *belos*, which also means a *threshold*: where a door is placed.

70   I chose that analogy carefully. It comes from the original French story about Lancelot; according to medieval scholar Joan Helm, one of the great neo-Platonic works of the Middle Ages. And by neo-Platonic, she means a Greek thought and spirituality seemingly onside with Christianity but actually deeply opposed to it.

71   Tehillim 2:12 at *www.chabad.org*

72   See, for example, 1 Samuel 10:1, when Samuel kisses Saul to symbolise Saul's being appointed as the ruler of Israel.

73   The Aramaic nashiyn, *wives*, is said to derive from 'enash, *man, mankind*, which is derived from 'enowsh, *mortal, man, men, mankind*, which is in turn derived from 'anash, *weak, sick, incurable*. Perhaps it is. But permit me a moment of scepticism to raise the possibility that nashiyn, *wives*, is related to nasu, *married*, and is actually derived from *nasa', to lift up*

74   Ephesians 5:19-20 and 6:18

75   See http://bit.ly/OCXL26

76   Deuteronomy 7:7— *The Lord did not set His affection on you and choose you because you were more numerous than other peoples, for you were the fewest of all peoples*

       Psalm 91:14— *'Because he loves Me,' says the Lord, 'I will rescue him; I will protect him, for he acknowledges My name.'*

       Isaiah 38:17— *Surely it was for my benefit that I suffered such anguish. In Your love You kept me from the pit of destruction; You have put all my sins behind Your back.*

77   As it says in Ephesians 2:10 where the word usually translated *workmanship* or *masterpiece* actually comes from the Greek for poem. For a fuller treatment of this concept of God's people as His poetry, see *God's Poetry: The Identity and Destiny Encoded in Your Name.*

78   Philippians 3:5-6 NIV

79 Personally I suspect 616 and 666 of being in this mix, too.

80 Positioned (not surprisingly) to divide the use of *chara* into a 3:1 ratio

81 Plutarch—the high priest of Delphi—relates that their abhorrence had to do with the dismemberment of the Egyptian god, Osiris, however his explanation seems quite odd since the Pythagoreans were noted for *not* being religious— that is, for not worshipping a multiplicity of gods, but sticking to one. (Similarly, the Christians of the first century—and the Jews before them—were regarded as atheists because they did not worship a pantheon of gods.) And 'The One,' however, was not Osiris, but Apollo. Most of what we know about the legend of Isis and Osiris actually comes from Plutarch (which, if we look for a modern equivalent is essentially the same as relying on the Dalai Lama for the main beliefs of the Shinto religion) and this should make us very wary indeed of his comments about 17 since that number had already firmly established itself as *the* favourite amongst the writers of a small sect of Judaism, variously known as followers of The Way or as Christians.

82 Clearly inspiring the stanza in Milton's *On Time*:

The Oracles are dumm,
No voice or hideous humm
Runs through the arched roof in words deceiving.
Apollo from his shrine
Can no more divine,
With hollow shreik the steep of Delphos leaving.
No nightly trance, or breathed spell,
Inspire's the pale–ey'd Priest from the prophetic cell

(Kenneth Gross, *Each Heav'nly Close: Mythologies and Metrics in Spenser and the Early Poetry of Milton*, PMLA, Vol. 98, No. 1, 1983)

83 Moreover, the Greek word for *musician* has a gematria of 101.

84 A passage from the narrative poem *Cligés* by Chrétien de Troyes is an exemplar of why the author of *Sir Gawain and the Green Knight* equated neo–Platonism with anti–Christian sentiment: Fenice, the Empress of Constantinople, on confessing her love for her husband's nephew, reveals that, despite all appearances to the contrary, her marriage has never been consummated. She explains the Emperor has drunk a magic potion which gives him the illusion of nightly sexual satisfaction. Fenice of course wants to be with her true love and has hatched a plan. She does not, however, propose following the example of Tristan and Iseult, but suggests instead faking her own death. (Shades of *Romeo and Juliet* but without the tragedy.) She quotes St. Paul's advice to Timothy in advocating this course of action, pointing out that the apostle taught that those who found it too hard to remain chaste should be careful to arrange their affairs so that no one finds out what they're doing. Be discreet and so avoid criticism and slander. (*Cligés, 5306–5312*)

Now, of course, Paul said nothing of the kind. Chrétien thus twisted the words of the epistle regarding sexual morality so the emphasis was not on remaining chaste but on avoiding a bad reputation so that the church is not impugned. Not only that, his magic-dabbling Scripture-perverting heroine was called Fenice, a name clearly derived from 'phoenix'. This mythical bird allegedly lived 500 or 540 years and renewed itself in the fires of its own funeral pyre. Because of its resurrection through the flames, it was understood throughout the Middle Ages as a type of Christ. If this wasn't enough of an attack on a traditional Christian motif, to add mathematical insult to theological injury, Fenice, lying in a death-like coma, is attacked by three doctors from Salerno who see through her ruse and begin to assault her on Line 5940—which at 540 x 11 is a multiple of one of the traditional lifetimes of the phoenix—and set her on a fiery pyre on Line 5994—or 54 x 111.

Did Chrétien know that 111 was a number associated with the City of God and the reign of justice and peace? According to Joan Helm's analysis of *Erec et Enide*, yes, he most certainly did.

85 An acre, described by experts as the 'most intriguing' of ancient measures, is defined as a rectangular area 1 chain in width by 1 furlong in length. A chain is the length of a cricket pitch: so an acre is a cricket pitch wide by 10 cricket pitches long!

86 The ratio of the area of the City with suburbs to the City without suburbs is $5000^2:4500^2$ or 1.2345679:1. Confirming that this is not simply a coincidence is the number 1056, also associated with Erec, and which in scriptural context corresponds to the length of one of the angelic 'reeds' used to measure the heavenly City. These were six cubits in length, a cubit in this case understood as being the standard (and not the royal) measure of 17.6 inches.

To wrap up the symbolism, Chrétien used the number 1742 to point out the incomparable harmony of the marriage of two such beautiful figures, a perfection in the case of Enide that so stuns the character of King Arthur that he exclaims she can only come from the meeting place of heaven and earth.

87 Nesher by itself is 550. Richard McGough relates nesher to *sar*, prince or ruler, and to government and, in Greek, the law. Because of the words of the angel to Jacob in Genesis 32:28—*Thy name shall be called no more Jacob, but **Israel**: for as a prince hast thou power with God and with men, and hast prevailed*—he also suggests the word prince is embedded in the 'sr' of Israel and that these concepts are all related.

88 So much for the idea that they thought the earth was flat. As CS Lewis and many others pointed out, more people believed in a flat earth in the nineteenth century than ever did during the Middle Ages.

89 Helm quotes other important numbers in her analysis and includes other ways 3168 was used to show how the sphere of the Moon is brought down to touch the Earth, thus rolling up part of the heavens and eliminating the 'infernal

regions' in between where the demons of the air were said to dwell. There was more than one way to bring about a union of heaven and earth using 3168

90   http://www.ericmetaxas.com/blog/communion-on-the-moon-july-20th-1969/

91   And by 'end of the century' I, of course, mean 31 December 2000. Because there was no year 0, the first century ran from 1 AD to 100 AD, the second century from 101 AD to 200 AD and so on.

92   1111 of course is the City of God motif and 303 is the golden ratio of 490 which makes it a motif of both truth and mercy. Permit me a 'wow!' moment.

It can also be a summation of 490+231+153+540, all of these symbolic numbers. 490 is seventy times seven, a metaphor for forgiveness. 153 appears in John 21 as the number of fish which were caught in the net on the third occasion Jesus appeared to his disciples after He rose from the dead. It was anciently known, well before the time of Jesus, as 'the number of the fish' and was part of a famous geometrical figure. It is the 17th triangular number and is the first number which can be 'resurrected' from the skeleton of its own digits under a 'Trinity function'. (For what all this means, see Anne Hamilton, *The Winging Word*, Phares 2009) 231 is the 21st triangular number and is regarded as symbolic of the Trinity since 21 is also a triangular number (the 6th) and 6 is also a triangular number. It's also regarded as a 'resurrection number' since the sum of its factors is 153. Yet another 'resurrection number' in this mix is 540, so regarded because it was considered to be the number of years in the lifetime of a phoenix, which was an emblem of Christ since it is reborn in the flames of its own funeral pyre.

93   The 111th day from the end of the year is right after September 11. This day is now historically significant in world history as commemorating the destruction of the Twin Towers in New York. According to Jonathan Cahn's remarkable book, *The Harbinger*, the day after September 11, 2001, has many spiritual overtones. However, these are to do more with breaking than with keeping covenant.

94   The Hebrew words for 'gave him tithes' is 1112; for 'into his hand gave tithes' is 1112 and for 'the most high God who has delivered your enemies' is 1111.

95   Patterson, like many Jewish scholars, uses the spelling 'elokim' not 'elohim'.

96   See for instance, http://bibleapps.com/hebrew/853.htm or

http://www.hebrew4christians.com/Names_of_G-d/Trinity/trinity.html

97   Two letters are required because two is the minimum number of witnesses required by the Law. Deuteronomy 19:15 sets out the requirement for more than a single witness. Other passages such as Deuteronomy 30:19 indicate that the witnesses do not always have to be human, thus using letters as witnesses is consistent with the idea that the whole of creation, even what modern

science would class as inanimate, is in some sense 'alive'. It is worth noting that letters are also numbers in Hebrew and that they can serve as witnesses.

98   http://www.tnnonline.net/faq/A/Alef_Tav_Yeshua_as_the.pdf

99   To be honest, I find it truly astonishing that it is so obvious—far more obvious than it would have been in the past. Our presentday decimal system makes things easy to see at a glance. Even the system of Roman numerals with which many people are still familiar renders 1111 as MCXI which doesn't have quite the exquisite run of the decimals.

100   See my book, *The Singing Silence*.

101   See *http://homepage.virgin.net/vernon.jenkins/First_Princs.htm* which also shows John 1:1 encodes an astonishingly accurate value for the transcendental and irrational number, e.

102   Bishop, L. M., *Words, Stones and Herbs – The Healing Word in Medieval and Early Modern England*, Syracuse University Press, 2007

103   Such as *Lamentations* which is entirely poetic in format and designed with a very careful mathematical structure. The first, second, fourth and fifth laments all contain 22 verses, reflecting the number of letters in the Hebrew alphabet. The first two laments contain verses of three lines; the fourth has verses of two lines; and in the fifth each verse contains a single line. The first four laments are alphabetic acrostics. In the first, second and fourth, each numbered verse begins with the appropriate letter of the Hebrew alphabet. The third lament is distinctive and consists of 22 three-line units (like laments 1 and 2), in it the three lines of each unit follow an alphabetic sequence.

104   1 Corinthians 3:9

105   The π of Genesis 1:1 is not totally outside the realm of possibility, though excessively unlikely to have been planned by the writer. The natural logarithm, the *e* of John 1:1, however is too incredible to have been deliberately planned by the writer. The fact John 1:1 builds on Genesis 1:1 and *e* and π are related through what many mathematicians consider the most beautiful equation of all time—$e^{i\pi} + 1 = 0$—suggests to me that this is the point at which the Holy Spirit took over completely.

106   'The Groupist ignores the history of Christianity, and regards the system of the Church as too apparently ineffective to command acceptance. He moves at a stride from the Age of Apostles to the present time, and assumes that the centuries of Christian experience have nothing to teach him. Surely this is a position which cannot seriously be defended.' *The Oxford Groups; The Charge Delivered At The Third Quadrennial Visitation Of His Diocese Together With An Introduction*, Herbert Hensley Henson, D.D. (the Bishop of Durham), 1933

107   2 Peter 1:5 NIV

108   Luke 2:51 ESV

109   Jeff Benner, *His Name is One.*

110   http://bit.ly/VEi4KD

111   There's actually an English word which perpetuates the very same idea: *cardinal.* Derived from the Latin, *cardo*, hinge, the senior officials of the Catholic Church are entrusted with electing a pope—as has recently happened for Francis I. Lawyers of the Church make the point that, in fact, all members of the clergy and laity are essentially cardinals with the right to elect the pope. Almost a thousand years ago in 1059, Pope Nicholas II established the principle that all the people had the right to be involved in such an election. However because no one has ever figured out a practical means of implementing this directive, this particular aspect of canon law has languished for almost a millennium. (*http://www.eurekastreet.com.au/article.aspx?aeid=35188*)

A final note: in my efforts to ensure this is a work of numerical literary art with a consistent mathematical signature and word-number integration, I would like to point out there are 111 endnotes of 5555 words. The 111 endnotes were intentional but the word count was not. But it was so close when I checked it and such a small matter to adjust it, that it seemed right to do so.

About the author

According to her mother, Anne Hamilton was born asking, 'Why?' Many rabbinical sources note that the Hebrew word for *question*, shelah, contains the name of God, El. God, they therefore say, is in the question. With such a warrant, her curiosity is wide-ranging and encompasses names and their meanings, the fusion of words and numbers in ancient literature, and Hebrew thought. A former mathematics teacher, she works for a national radio network as a writer and editor.

www.fire-of-roses.com/wp

Epilogue

A Few Words Regarding the Cover

It looks odd, doesn't it? A daffodil on fire doesn't exactly shout 'armour of God', does it?

In the years while this book was coming to fruition, I searched carefully for the 'perfect' cover. One with symbolic meaning that matched the first book in this series. I prayed about it a lot—asking the Holy Spirit to make the choice, not me. A very dangerous move, as it transpired.

Eventually I chose a soft focus medieval scene of a knight on a horse in a misty field and, in order to persuade my publisher about the perfection of my choice, I decided to buy the stock photo. Although I'd checked on it just the day previously, it was suddenly unavailable. It had disappeared from every selection list.

I was startled and puzzled. Was this a bizarre spiritual attack?

After a lot of prayer over pictures of Roman soldiers, random pieces of armour and stylised heraldic shields, the illustration that impressed itself on me time and time again was a daffodil on fire. The Holy Spirit seemed to say, 'This is My choice.'

How could I convince my publisher when I couldn't really convince myself? Eventually we went with it—dubiously, I must admit. On the day after the first print run was ordered, a day too late to make changes to the text, I discovered the symbolism of a daffodil in Hebrew.

The 'rose of Sharon' is believed to be a daffodil–like narcissus, twice mentioned in Scripture. Sharon is a word connected with both body armour and righteousness, while the word for rose, havatzelet, has been translated overshadowed by God's love. Didn't I say Paul was a die-hard romantic?

Here, in the allusion to the word sharon—a single word which encapsulates both breastplate and righteousness—is also that final threshold pun I was sure we were missing. Paul has encoded a reference to sha'ar for gate.

Yet again we have a sense of the corporate body Paul continually talks about: gates belong to a city, more than a house. Gates were synonymous in Hebrew thinking with judgment since in ancient times, judges delivered their verdicts at the gates of a city. Ideally of course the judges would pronounce justly and righteously.

What a complex and intricate allusion!

However, what intrigued me in it was the reference to a flower. Were there others? Had the Holy Spirit chosen the cover to point to something deeper?

Rather than try to amend the hard-wrought numerical literary design of the present text to add this information, I decided on this epilogue with its 490 words. I hope you'll forgive its unusual nature and placement. Just think of it like those tiny teasers you find inserted in the credits of a movie.

So if you'd like to come in search of six other wildflowers, seven gemstones and a musical formulation, be sure to join me in *God's Pageantry*, the next book in this series.

Anne Hamilton

Postscript and a small wave offering of a kind:
John is the treasurer of the writers' group I attend. Being financially minded, he noticed a string-of-ones I'd overlooked in discussing 2011. He wrote: *'The Commonwealth Bank issues a 12-digit receipt number for every internet transaction. A recent receipt was N081132875170. The receipt number N011111111111 was issued on 11/11/2011.'*

CPSIA information can be obtained
at www.ICGtesting.com
Printed in the USA
BVHW080712200620
581892BV00002B/248